place, being, resonance

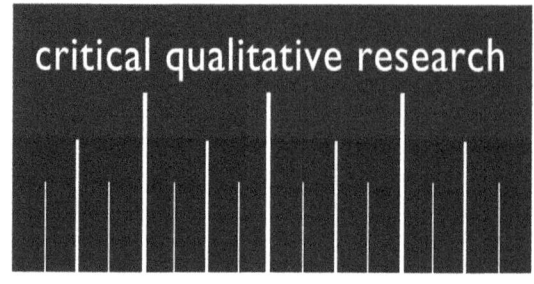

CRITICAL ISSUES FOR LEARNING AND TEACHING

Shirley R. Steinberg and Gaile S. Cannella
Series Editors

Vol. 18

The Critical Qualitative Research series
is part of the Peter Lang Education list.
Every volume is peer reviewed and meets
the highest quality standards for content and production.

PETER LANG
New York • Bern • Frankfurt • Berlin
Brussels • Vienna • Oxford • Warsaw

michael w. derby

place, being, resonance

a critical ecohermeneutic approach to education

PETER LANG
New York • Bern • Frankfurt • Berlin
Brussels • Vienna • Oxford • Warsaw

Library of Congress Cataloging-in-Publication Data
Derby, Michael W.
Place, being, resonance: a critical ecohermeneutic approach to education / Michael W. Derby.
pages cm. — (Critical qualitative research; vol. 18)
Includes bibliographical references.
1. Environmental education—Philosophy. 2. Ecolinguistics.
3. Hermeneutics. I. Title.
GE70.D47   363.70071—dc23   2015017297
ISBN 978-1-4331-2731-1 (hardcover)
ISBN 978-1-4331-2730-4 (paperback)
ISBN 978-1-4539-1656-8 (e-book)
ISSN 1947-5993

Bibliographic information published by **Die Deutsche Nationalbibliothek**.
Die Deutsche Nationalbibliothek lists this publication in the "Deutsche Nationalbibliografie"; detailed bibliographic data are available on the Internet at http://dnb.d-nb.de/.

Back cover photo by Bob Jickling

© 2015 Peter Lang Publishing, Inc., New York
29 Broadway, 18th floor, New York, NY 10006
www.peterlang.com

All rights reserved.
Reprint or reproduction, even partially, in all forms such as microfilm, xerography, microfiche, microcard, and offset strictly prohibited.

For James E. Stewart and in memory of Howard W. Derby, grandfathers.

And for all the teachings I have been gifted by stones, grandfathers.

contents

acknowledgments	ix
some notes on terminology	xi
introduction—how to love black snow *by David W. Jardine*	xv
chapter one—this is the mystery: meaning	1
chapter two—mycelia & the hermeneutics beneath us	18
chapter three—the ecopoetics of education	28
chapter four—metaphor & thinking with *this* bird	43
chapter five—inoculating hermeneutics: Heidegger substrates	60
chapter six—inoculating hermeneutics: Gadamer substrates	85
chapter seven—hermeneutics deep in the clearcut	97
chapter eight—re-indigenization & the ethics of home-making	111
chapter nine—conclusion: a tree of meaning	131
references	143

acknowledgments

How does one acknowledge the confluence of forces giving rise to a thing such as this? Mark Fettes played a formative and sustaining role and it is an honour to acknowledge his extraordinary brilliance as a scholar, his radical spirit as a comrade, and his thoughtful and unremitting support as a friend. Likewise, this would never have been without years of rich conversation, camaraderie and multifarious support from Sean Blenkinsop. I walked for a long time lost in this life, looking for mentors and never expecting to find any —I am glad to have found you (now we can be lost together). I have also been blessed to find my peoples in the newfangled ultra-revolutionary assemblage of ecophilosopher-poets at Simon Fraser University including: Laura Piersol, John Telford, Vicki Kelly, Jodi MacQuarrie, Veronica Hotton, Michael Caulkins, Nora Timmerman, Carlos Ormond and Chloe Humphreys, word up. Thanks for the conversations, and the silent times in the forest.

Revelry and transcendental buffoonery for everyone in the Imaginative Education Research Group. In particular, a respectable dollop of gratitude for Kieran Egan and heartfelt vibes for Gillian Judson, thank you for your important work and for keeping rhythm, wonder and radical epistemic doubt on the table. Also Kym Stewart, Natalia Gajdamaschko, Tim Waddington, Annabella Cant, Joeri Cant, Heesoon Bai, Ann Chinnery, and Michael Ling.

Four scholars fundamentally shaped the thinking in this work and over the past three years I have had the good fortune to meet all of them—each proving to be uniquely beautiful and wild. First and foremost, David Jardine, thank you for your boundless heart and for inspiring so many in this season of great untruth. I overheard one of your students say, "I did not even know what hermeneutics meant until I took this class, now it is all I think about." This work began when I was elicited by your writing—I wanted to think and write like that, to teach and be like that—now it is all I think about. The others are Jan Zwicky, Robert Bringhurst and Tim Lilburn who taught me to recognize the identity of poetry and thinking and how to attend to the resonant ecology of things. I am forever grateful for your work, your words, your poetry, your music. A thousand little fungi-shaped bells ring for you.

Fields of fierce green to all the feral creatures in education and beyond, especially those I have been fortunate enough to connect with: David Greenwood, Ramsey Affifi, Derek Rasmussen, Bob Jickling, Joseph Henderson, Kyle Clarke, Greg Scutt, Karen McIver, Leesa Fawcett, Joshua Russell, Rebecca Martusewicz, Richard Kahn, Clayton Pierce, Paul Hart, Phillip Payne, Catherine Hart, Marcia McKenzie, Jackie Seidel, Nicholas Stanger, Greg Lowan-Trudeau, David Hursh, Constance Russell, Julia Ostertag, Alexa Scully, Mitch McLarnon, Sarah Stapleton, Enid Elliot, Marlene Power, Sarah DesRoches, Emily Sadowski, Liz Jackson, Clarence Joldersma, Tyson Lewis, Eduardo Duarte, Jade Ho, Stef Block and Dale Martelli, just to name a few. Much gratitude for scholarship support and inspiration from those in the Philosophy of Education Society of Australasia, including John Ozolins, David Beckett, John Quay, Jayne White, Peter Roberts, Tina Besley, Nesta Divine and Michael A. Peters, among others. During the writing of this book I have also been the grateful beneficiary of research funds from the Social Sciences and Humanities Research Council of Canada. Finally, much respect to series editor Shirley R. Steinberg and a deferent headnod to the late Joe Kincheloe.

To my family and friends, who have had to endure my becoming, this is what I found. *Here*. Much gratitude to my mother Morag for her immeasurable love; to my father Allan for taking me into the wilderness and showing me how to live kindly; and to my sister Jolaine who is joy and laughing and caring. Both my grandmothers returned to the earth during the writing of this book, Grandma Betsy and Grandma Clare, I love you, I miss you. To my beloved T'selpinek, thank you for coming with me this far, we are only just beginning. You are *still* my favourite mystery, my heart will ponder you forever. To my little Toby, thank you for teaching me to love small things and for watching over me all these years. Lastly, I would like to acknowledge the flesh these words dance upon, the rivers in our veins and mycelia in our minds, the vibrant processes and rhythms that resonate *beneath* all this. May we learn to listen.

some notes on terminology

A note on the use of "we" and other third person pronouns. I often tell students that "we" is the most dangerous word in the English language. Who is *we*? When I use "we" or any other third person pronoun I am usually referring to those immersed in modern Western ways of thinking. I say this not to further align myself with this tradition, but out of respect for the alterity of primitive communities, Indigenous communities, communities of the Eastern traditions, more-than-human communities and all other communities who have lived and learned, and continue to live and learn, other than *we* do.

A note on the use of the term "Indigenous." I would like to avoid reproducing the colonial logic of "pan-Indianism," which is to say, speaking about Indigenous peoples as if they are a homogenous group with uniform social practices, histories and ontological orientations. With that said, I will respectfully speak of "worldviews," "knowledges," and "ways of knowing" that emerge from the wisdom traditions of "Indigenous peoples." To this end I will evoke the definition provided by Gregory Cajete (1994). The term Indigenous will apply broadly to the many traditional and tribally oriented groups of peoples who are identified with a specific place or region and whose cultural traditions continue to reflect an inherent environmental orientation and sense of sacred ecology. The term Indigenous will also describe the culturally based forms of education that are not primarily rooted in modern Western educational philosophy and methodology (p. 15).

The poet produces the beautiful by fixing his attention on something real. It is the same with the act of love. To know that this man who is hungry and thirsty really exists as much as I do—that is enough, the rest follows of itself.

The authentic and pure values—truth, beauty and goodness—in the activity of a human being are the result of one and the same act, a certain application of the full attention to the object.

Teaching should have no aim but to prepare, by training the attention, for the possibility of such an act. All the other advantages of instruction are without interest.

—Simone Weil, *Gravity and Grace*

introduction
how to love black snow

DAVID W. JARDINE

Despite the likely alien and awkward feel of the concepts involved, we might, when hearing a sutra, experience a quite innocent sense of wonder—a brief moment of almost childlike, delightful surprise, perhaps colored by a subtle tone of promise and potential. In line with the teachings set out in this book, we might say that just such a brief clearing within simple, unprepared wonder is what constitutes the awakening of faith in the Great Vehicle.
> From the "Translators' Introduction" to *Ornament of the Great Vehicle Sutras: Maitreya's Mahayanasutralamakara* (Doctor, 2014, p. vii)

Now little riverbed stones impress upon my bare feet the aggregate intelligence of form and fit, particular trees stand tall in my memory as pedagogically significant, the cheap yellow paint on my pencil peels and reveals *flesh*—what kind of mushrooms are these? From somewhere deep within the inquiry, beneath the words—*how is it possible!*—a world approaches. (p. 2)
> From chapter one—this is the mystery: meaning

This book is worth every moment of while it takes to read it. It must be read as carefully as mushrooms that always just might be poisonous even if delicious, just might be nourishing even if acrid. We are in a fix—pedagogically, ecologically, in body and mind and otherwise—and it's going to take some doing to even start undoing this fix.

The object of concern in this beautiful book is grave and imminent—the tear of flesh that is surely coming in these ecologically sorrowful times. michael's book is rife with soaring, awakening insight into the often ignored, often trivialized and romanticized, nature of our ecological intimacy, our earthly being beyond the confines of the all too human. And it couples these insights with detailed and careful thought to the pedagogy of these matters and to long and tangled histories of human images and thinking in which we have "b[ou]nd ourselves without a rope" (Loy, 2010, p. vii).

Read this book slowly and repeatedly. That is what it needs and deserves. If you read it too fast, the pull of the gravity and imminence of our circumstances will only increase. Read slowly, the pull starts to lessen, and we can then slowly start to see where we are, what has happened to us and our kin, what we have done, what we might now do.

Hurry will only lead to panic that is distracting and of no use. It will only tighten the knots and the tangle and the confusion.

Here, right off the bat is one great gift of this book. We hurry.

And that last sentence can be read too fast. We hurry, and when our circumstances become dire, we react by accelerating, with little or no understanding of how our hurry is profoundly complicit in increasing our panic, thus increasing our hurry, and so on.

It is no accident that Buddhists characterize the deepest human afflictions as caught up in a Wheel.

The spell of this ever-accelerating wheeling must be broken. Great and increasingly loud and monstrous hallucinations about how we might Save The Earth (capitalized, and then in all caps, and then bolded, and then in a bigger pitch, and so on) must stop. This just increases the spellbinding.

In its stead, awakening, brief clearings, little riverbed stones and particular trees.

This book has been of great use and great remind to me in understanding a school I visited last week, listening to and watching French Immersion Grade One children couple together found words and posting them for all to see—and then up goes this accidental couplet, *neige/noir*, "black snow," and how we all gasped a bit at the beckoning incomprehensibility of it: the feel of a world approaching, of aggregate intelligence, of language living instead of dead, and of the warm presence of us huddled together over this classroom happenstance. So momentary, but just because of this, the true weal of words is felt approaching and whooshing overhead.

We duck and giggle. In brief.

Neige noir. I must remember this.

This isn't a big deal, this. It's a small one. One among many pleasures in this book is that, read the right way, it is full of such clear and clearing messages

Introduction xvii

about commonplace and everyday events inside and outside of commonplace and everyday classrooms with commonplace and everyday children and adults and the territories in which they might meet their more-than-human kin. It is about how we might make schools not just *livable* and *sustainable* but *beautiful* and *wise*. It is not just *about* poetry (chapter three) or *about* metaphor (chapter four) but demands that:

> here, where it seems impossible
> that one life even matters (Wallace, 1987, p. 111)

Here, we seek the feel of mycelial pulls:

> right now, in the midst of things, *this*
> and *this* (p. 111)

This book asks me to stop over things, to stoop, to think. "With *this* bird" (chapter four). I am so relieved to say that this book is *not* about "environmental education" as some sort of subject area (usually a sub-division of Science Education or Outdoor Education or both) among others inside or outside of schools. This literal minded image of environmental education simply abandons the rest of our human inheritance and of the lives of teachers and students to countless ecological disasters, one worksheet after the other.

Instead, this: *All of our thinking and being and imagining is ecological.* All knowledge entrusted to teachers and students in schools comes with place and inhabitation and faces and tales—*fields* of wonder that call for the sort of thinking proper to such fields and their cultivation and care. This is an ancient Aristotelian reminder of *mensuratio ad rem*: thinking which finds its proper measure, not in the methods of human approach, but rather in the thing being thought:

> Thinking is not a means to gain knowledge. Thinking cuts furrows in the soil of Being. About 1875, Nietzsche once wrote (Grossoktav, WW XI, 20): "Our thinking should have a vigorous fragrance, like a wheatfield on a summer's night." How many of us today still have the senses for that fragrance? (Heidegger, 1971, p. 70).

From the beginning of chapter two:

> Occasionally, we may happen upon the fruiting bodies of this living, subterranean entanglement (if we live, or make time to go, or are taken to the places where fungi

still bloom, and if we pay attention) and only then do we become aware of the vibrant webwork beneath us and, perhaps, if our earthly connection has not been severed or schooled out of us, we are reminded of the interdependent ethos of a "humus filled" existence. (p. 38)

We, too, are fruiting bodies, as are Pythagoras and Andromeda and Coyote and place value, and this is no more and no less a metaphor than it is of fungi. Coyote always arrives with earthly connections and subterranean entanglements. And when you place something in a place, that place itself is not just an empty, abstract spot, but has a value (Latin *valere*, two meanings of which are "be strong, be well" [Online Etymological Dictionary]) that affects how to think about what happens to what has been placed there. Change the strength and well being of the place and things in that place change. My work could not have become what it did had I not lived in these Foothills. Place value.

Simple! Mathematics and its Roman and Arabic numeric roots are forms of ecological awareness, of locales and ancestors and relations and imagining. As a Grade Six student once told me, of course Roman numerals have no place value, because Rome was an Empire, and every place it went was Rome—"the vibrant webwork beneath us."

"The way we treat a thing can sometimes change its nature" (Hyde, 1983, p. iii), and we must not simply go outside (although we must, we must) and abandon everything left inside the school walls. This is the tough, exhilarating work that this book asks readers to practice right in the midst of the circumstances we face. *Here*. Grade One. If it can come to be treated the right way, for its fragrances. If we don't treat it that way, our sense for this fragrance becomes uncultivated, unpracticed, dimmed and distant. Its loss of fragrance and our nose for it rise and fall in concert. Thus, this book lays out a bit of a rescue mission, to learn to read even little Grade One word searches as eco-poetic, eco-pedagogical gestures, to become studied and still enough to stop panicking and let ourselves remember how both right-angled triangles and the curves of vines around a tree *both* become *more* radiant in each other's presence. Hans-Georg Gadamer (2007) calls this, in an indirect way, an experience of beauty. Each reads the other out into the open and releases it from its literal self-absorption and self-containedness. In each other's presence, each becomes exquisite and irreplaceable in the fullness of things and their ways. Treated properly, each is radiant, lighting up the dependently co-arising place of its residing, its strength and well-being, its place value. "We should apply this to *every* phenomenon" (Tsongkhapa, 2005, p. 182), our "selves" included.

Introduction xix

Hermeneutics deep in the clearcut (chapter seven). Inoculation (chapters five and six). Re-indigenization and home-making (chapter eight)—perhaps overall we are dealing with the ability to read properly, with a honed and practiced sense of place and proper proportion, with enough studied memory and experience so that the "resonant ecology of things" can be sensed ringing in the air. We must allow ourselves the hard labor of this repeated and perennial task of recovery, of waking up, again, in search of brief clearings.

Frankly, there is great joy to be had here, but it has got an ecological sting: "Everything is teaching you. Isn't this so? Can you just get up and walk away so easily now?"(Chah, n.d., p. 5).

There are two intertwining paths in this book, one more immediately pleasing than the other. More than any other book in recent memory (I might put Don Domanski's *Bite Down Little Whisper* [2013] alongside), this book feels and writes and speaks up out of the lift that comes when we step aside from our heavy inheritance and undo its cloak and instead wander, wilder, with stones underfoot and the duty of noticing. It is equally easy to recoil, as it is to rejoice in the deep experience of our conspiracy with trees and other terranean and subterranean entanglements. Coming still enough to experience for myself such dependency is, as michael shows in great detail, deliciously, properly and repeatedly humiliating. With practice, you get used to it. "It is somewhat difficult to establish, but once you are used to it, it will be like meeting an old acquaintance" (Kongtrul, 2002, p. 67). In such meetings, our hearts become undone.

This book thus speaks about acts of true teaching and learning in ways that lift and open the heart despite its sorrows, but not in order to turn away to some vaguely stupid Ecological Romance or equally distracting Ecological Panic. No, this lift allows *those very sorrows* to be sung in words and harmonies with ravens and stones and trees, and not just suffered in silence and isolation.

Neige noir and our huddling over it.

"Oh sorrow" (Seidel, 2014, p. 112).

"Hush, child" (Latremouille, 2014, p. 30). Do not panic.

Deep ecological stillness and experience—persistent, repeated, generous, patient, persevering—are vital to beginning to undo our fix, but they are not sufficient. There is another path in this book that gives heart and courage. It stares dead-on, articulately, and in great detail, into the inheritances of thinking and imagining that have helped get us into this fix. How have schools become so often so deadly and boring and afraid? How has literacy lost its ear for orality? How have the wise ghosts of the land underfoot become lost from memory?

How has beauty fled, and why, and what happens if we raise our kids in a world without ears, without ghosts, without beauty? This is the second path, which is at once the same path. *We need to study* in ways that return our living from its embroilment in unearthly fantasies and fears. Undoing ourselves from the fix we have inherited is going to take some doing. *Our study of our circumstances is going to have to be as complex and as difficult and as entailed as those circumstances themselves.*

There is no way around this and its great ironies. We humans, having disgraced and desecrated the more-than-human world (and, to our shame, the human one as well), have an all too human task facing us. We must seek wisdom. We must think clearly and without fear and consequent animal panics. As per hermeneutic insight, seeing the world and our fix only in light of and as an outcome of its imminent and grave impingement on us blocks us from seeing *it* as it is, as it stands there, in its own repose, "over and above our wanting and doing" (Gadamer, 1989, p. xxviii). It takes wisdom to escape our selves and the world that then appears only in light of those worried selves and our projections and fears and repressions. We must break our reflection in the water. We must come to, not in order to turn away from the spell, but towards it, now, finally, a bit awoken and more alert.

"You can't get anywhere without reading a yak's load of books" (Tsongkhapa, 2004, p. 219). One must cultivate "an attentive ear for the language in which the thinking experiences of many generations has been sedimented, long before we begin to attempt our own thinking" (Gadamer, 1992, p. 18). Part of the work here in this book is unraveling how our current ecological concern is, at least in part, a function of how so many of these generations have cocooned themselves (and therefore us, our language, our inheritances, our schools, our teaching and learning) and long-since lost an Earthly measure of things. And so many of these generations have demanded of those they met that they, too, must lose such measure and its language, its culture, its places. These circumstances are complicated, historically, culturally, philosophically, linguistically, spiritually. They involve colonialism, gender, dreams of heaven and progress and monstrous hopes for mastery over the world, and on and on and on. They include institutional codifications and market economies and media distractions and the "you're either for us or against us" logic of much political wind. We can step away, momentarily, from this tough work, as I often must, seeking the relief of ravens and wood to split and tomato seedlings on the sill. But simply stepping away leaves our path still blocked.

Introduction xxi

This is why this book leans heavily into the phenomenological and hermeneutic traditions of Edmund Husserl, Martin Heidegger (see especially chapter five), and my old love, Hans-Georg Gadamer (see especially chapter six). I've taught a graduate course in the University of Calgary's Faculty of Education on Gadamer's *Truth and Method* over twenty-five times, and it has proven to be true, over and over again, a hermeneutic adage: "[the world] compels over and over, and the better one knows it, the *more* compelling it is. This is not a matter of mastering an area of study" (Gadamer, 2007, p. 115). This tradition, at its best and most vital, lends its attention to the life world, the world as lived, the living world. This tradition—part of the very Eurocentric orbit that has caused so much of our fix—seeks the break of the spell, seeks the Trickster who knows the trick, seeks waking up, it seeks beauty and repose, it seeks to understand "what happens to us over and above our wanting and doing" (Gadamer, 1989, p. xxviii)—all out from constructivist cocoons and somnambulant projects and delusions.

Here is where this book becomes slightly magnificent, because the author does not wish to simply swallow whole this tradition of phenomenological and hermeneutic philosophy because it, too and of course, contains calcified and hardened elements of precisely the unearthliness that has gotten us into the fix we are in in the first place. What the author makes crystal clear is the need for what he brilliantly calls "ecohermeneutic inoculation."

> Ecohermeneutic inoculation in this respect is a deliquescent move—at once critical and remedial—that compels a tradition to reveal what it knows, what it has yet to teach, and where it needs to reconnect in order to remain in resonance with the world and our lives as they are now lived. In this sense, an ecohermeneutic imagination is…concerned with…"salvaging" and revitalizing these philosophic substrates to bring them to bear on ecological pedagogy in a more-than-human world. (p. 60-61)

I do adore the fact that I had to look up the word "deliquescent." This is one of the leisures (Latin *schola*) of study. Unidentified words, like unidentified mushrooms, come to be experienced ecstatically, as a trail with beckonings along it. And, as with mushrooms, getting the etymology wrong can make us lose our way: "from Latin *deliquescere* 'to melt away,' from *de-* + *liquescere* 'to melt,' from *liquere* 'to be liquid'" (On-Line Etymological Dictionary). This is why we learn to spell. Because if we don't, the spell gets lost, the threads of ancestral memory get cut, and we no longer have any aid in finding our way.

We become lost, and, because of our loss, we eat mushrooms that are deadly. It is an ecological disaster.

Yes. Wait. Here. Got it! Deliquescence. Hermeneutics "makes the object and all its possibilities fluid" (Gadamer, 1989, p. 367) so that we can experience its living arising and living place in our lived experience and that of our dependents:

> All this has as its aim not simply philosophical erudition and the like. The aim of such meditations and work is the cultivation of the intimacy and immediacy of the experience of everyday life, here, as this next child draws breath over a text, here, where reading aloud and learning to pronounce can too often be treated as simply ordinary and commonplace. Not only is "wherever you are . . . a place of practice" (Tsongkhapa, 2004, p. 191). Tsongkhapa also insists (and this is a feature that distinguishes the Gelug tradition from other Buddhist lineages and makes ripe its affinity to hermeneutics), the purpose and object of study is *precisely* the deepening of practice itself. After all, "why would you determine one thing by means of study and reflection, and then, when you go to practice, practice something else?" (2000, p. 52). And this is why Gadamer insists that hermeneutics, with all its philosophical erudition and study, is "a practical philosophy" (2007a) with both theoretical and practical tasks (2007b). All those complex philosophical and historical twists and turns that typify his work are meant, in the end, to make us more susceptible to the beautiful abundance of things as we walk around in the world. (Jardine, 2015, p. 246)

"Texts are instructions for [the] practice" (Tsongkhapa, 2000, p. 52) of precisely paying more intimate and proper attention to the resonance. Don't worry. Study, properly practiced, will not ruin the *aesthesis* of ecological reveries, only their limited and limiting naiveties.

Study this book. It can help you become more alert and less afraid. It can provide the courage to face our circumstances full face and crack the facade that seems so grave and imminent and that beckons us to panic and retreat or to fall prey to useless, however understandable, ecological hysterics.

Come revel, then, and feel the amp of the sun increasing. I end this introduction with a sense of very strange relief. My own work is now being outlived, as michael ventures into many places that I have not been and many I have trouble going to without too much ache. My work belongs to a different time and place even though I'm in conspiracy with michael's words and better for his help.

This book, too, won't last forever. But it is, I believe, what is needed now.

Bragg Creek, Alberta, March 12, 2015

References

Chah, A. (n.d.). *Everything is teaching us.* Victoria AU: The Sangha. Bodhivana Monastery. Available for free download at: http://forestsanghapublications.org/viewAuthor.php?id=1

Doctor, T.H. (2014). Translators' introduction to *Ornament of the Great Vehicle Sutras: Maitreya's Mahayanasutralamakara* (pp. vii-xvi). Boston MA: Snow Lion.

Domanski, D. (2013). *Bite down little whisper.* London ON: Brick Books.

Gadamer, H.G (1989). *Truth and method.* New York, NY: Continuum Books.

Gadamer, H. G. (1992). *Hans-Georg Gadamer on education, poetry, and history: Applied hermeneutics.* (D. Misgeld & G. Nicholson Eds.) (L. Schmidt & M. Reuss, Trans.). Albany, NY: State University of New York.

Gadamer, H.G. (2007). From word to concept: The task of hermeneutics as philosophy. In *The Gadamer reader: A bouquet of later writings.* (R. Palmer, Trans. and Ed.) Evanston, IL: Northwestern University Press, pp. 108-120.

Gadamer, H.G. (2007a). Hermeneutics as practical philosophy. In *The Gadamer reader: A bouquet of later writings.* (R. Palmer, Trans. and Ed.). Evanston, IL: Northwestern University Press, pp. 227-246.

Gadamer, H.G. (2007b). Hermeneutics as a theoretical and practical task. In *The Gadamer reader: A bouquet of later writings.* (R. Palmer, Trans. and Ed.). Evanston, IL: Northwestern University Press, pp. 246-265.

Heidegger, M. (1971) *On the Way to Language.* New York: Harper and Row.

Hyde, L. (1983). *The gift: Imagination and the erotic life of property.* New York: Vintage Books.

Jardine, D. (2015). In praise of radiant beings. In D. Jardine, C. Gilham, & G. McCaffrey (2015). *On the pedagogy of suffering: Hermeneutic and Buddhist meditations.* New York, NY: Peter Lang Publishing.

Kongtrul, J. (2002). *Creation and completion.* Boston: Wisdom Publications.

Latremouille, J. (2014). *Feasting on whispers: Life writing towards a pedagogy of kinship.* Unpublished Master's Thesis, Werklund School of Education, University of Calgary.

Loy, D. (2010). *The world is made of stories.* Boston: Wisdom Publications.

On-line etymological dictionary. Accessed on-line at: www.etymologyonline.com.

Seidel, J. (2014). Hymn to the North Atlantic Right Whale. In J. Seidel & D. Jardine (2014). *Ecological pedagogy, Buddhist pedagogy, hermeneutic pedagogy: Experiments in a curriculum for miracles* (p. 11-2). New York: Peter Lang Publishing.

Tsongkhapa (2000). *The great treatise on the stages of the path to enlightenment (Lam rim chen mo).* Volume One. Ithaca NY: Snow Lion Publications.

Tsongkhapa (2004). *The great treatise on the stages of the path to enlightenment (Lam rim chen mo).* Volume Two. Ithaca NY: Snow Lion Publications.

Tsongkhapa (2005). *The six yogas of Naropa.* Ithaca NY: Snow Lion Publications.

Wallace, B. (1987). *The stubborn particulars of grace.* Toronto ON: McClellan and Stewart.

chapter one

this is the mystery: meaning

> Sun, moon, mountains and rivers are the writing of being, the literature of what-is. Long before our species was born, the books had been written. The library was here before we were. We live in it...
>
> When you think intensely and beautifully, something happens. That something is called poetry. If you think that way and speak at the same time, poetry gets in your mouth. If people hear you, it gets in their ears. If you think that way and write at the same time, then poetry gets written. But poetry *exists* in any case. The question is only: are you going to take part, and if so, how?
>
> (Bringhurst, 2006, p. 143)

The term *critical ecohermeneutics* has a nice ring. Clear and academic undertones issue from its obvious casting within the hermeneutic tradition. The *critical* suggests a resounding ethical concern, perhaps a tenor of the radical spirit of days past; the lingering vibes of bygone generations reminding us to remember refusal, renewal, relation. The *eco* suggests an expedient and timely retrofit; setting a new tone for sustainable and holistic ways of understanding in a world confronted by an escalading ecological crisis. Clear as a bell.

But a subtle subterranean tremble, a polyphonous intimation emanating from somewhere beneath its surface definition has given me pause. What is the meaning of *this* tremulous gesture? This field of compositions diffused with   voices, this decay
inoculated with
being?

Digging for possible interpretations has left me feeling strange, *elicited* (provoked, drawn forth, pierced) by the initiatory address of things. Now little riverbed stones impress upon my bare feet the aggregate intelligence of form and fit, particular trees stand tall in my memory as pedagogically significant, the cheap yellow paint on my pencil peels and reveals *flesh*—what kind of mushrooms are these? From somewhere deep within the inquiry, beneath the words—*how is it possible!*—a world approaches.

> Gadamer: A question presses itself upon us.
> Rilke: Not yours, a world's.[1]

Sometimes the question is vast and cerulean.

> ...[a sensible quality, like the color blue,] which is on the point of being felt sets a kind of muddled problem for my body to solve. I must find the attitude which will provide it with the means of becoming determinate, of showing up as blue; I must find the reply to a question which is obscurely expressed. And yet I do so only when I am invited by it; my attitude is never sufficient to make me really see blue or really touch a hard surface. The sensible gives back to me what I lent to it, but this is only what I took from it in the first place. As I contemplate the blue of the sky...I abandon myself to it and plunge into this mystery, it "thinks itself within me," I am the sky itself as it is drawn together and unified, and as it begins to exist for itself; my consciousness is saturated with this limitless blue... (Merleau-Ponty as cited in Abram, 1996, p. 54)

But contrary to the Western penchant for looking ever skywards for pure values, an ecohermeneutic attention is humbly drawn towards the earth. Here, walking a boreal forest path with a group of students, for example, a question emerges from rotting leaves and moss, pressing itself upon the attentive mind with a spellbinding crimson cap flecked with white. Such an encounter invariably rouses the standard taxonomical queries: "What kind of mushrooms are these?" *Amanita muscaria*, I believe, or fly agarics as they are commonly known. But a definitive name, a quick answer to an obscurely expressed question, can signal the terminal point of wonder. If we are willing to remain on what poet Don McKay called "the phenomenological edge" (2002, p. 60) and fix our attention on the particulars of this invitation, something happens. *Ah yes, now I remember, this.* But the sensible gives back only what is lent to it in the first place: first there must be a certain application of the full attention, a mycelial moment of connection, a gesture of love.

---

1   As cited in Jardine, 2006, p. 271, 274.

Chapter One

> Poetry *is* before it *begins* in a sense. Like stopping a person momentarily in their tracks with a poem they have happened to look at accidentally and they forget that they were to catch a bus somewhere and they look around and think: My God, I'm living in the world! (Snyder, 1980, pp. 18-19)

ৡ

In the classroom, questions tend to be a little more clearcut, and answers are expected to come quickly with a flash of raised hands and demonstrations of prescribed learning outcomes. And yet, even here, mycelial moments emerge to stop us in our tracks (from running our prescribed course, our curriculum). Teacher asks: "But what is *really* happening here in this story?" Little michael stares out the window, reflecting for a moment, and then—his face lighting up— he recognizes the *real* meaning, waylaying between the lines (*The true locus of hermeneutics*) (Gadamer, 2013, p. 306). Mind you, *real* does not imply *only*—teacher moves around the circle: "and what does everyone else think?" Meanwhile, out in the schoolyard, an autumn wind whispers between the children's voices...

> Both rise in excitement and play. The bell signals changes and little feet patter into position in the classroom. Inside, the door clicks gently shut, the wind disappears and the laughter and chatter are replaced by the anxious shuffling silence that awaits the future, a lesson in history. Silence yawns. But some desks are vacant. Three students burst into the room, the door bangs on its hinges, the result of a passionate opening. Deep breaths, sparkling eyes, flushed cheeks, a final intake...
> "Look what we found!"...the urgent rustling of waving fists filled with vibrant maple leaves. And, from the back of the room; "Why have those leaves turned red?" The question hangs. (Creeping Snowberry & Blenkinsop, 2010, p. 54)

Interpretive or hermeneutic traditions allow us to reflect upon the pedagogical significance of such individual moments of "fecundity" (Gadamer, 2013, p. 36). Bringing out these living, mycelial-like interweavings in their full, ambiguous, multivocal character is, as educational philosopher David Jardine has claimed, the task of hermeneutics (1998, p. 34). But first we must recognize that these sometimes wonderful and sometimes messy and ambiguous interweavings are really real, not distractions from more pressing curricular objectives or novel ornaments to embellish logico-mathematical forms of thinking. As Jardine maintains, the hermeneutic tradition reminds us that education, ecology and even mathematics are all at their best when organized around ideas of interrelatedness, generativity, ancestry, kinship, humility, wonder. In other words, good educators, like good hermeneutic philosophers and good poets (and, really, good scientists and mathematicians), must cultivate in themselves and in their students a sense of the living *interpretability of the world* (p. 1).

An ecohermeneutic approach to pedagogy thus encourages pausing momentarily in our tracks to consider, for example, a fistful of red leaves. To recognize the moment as pedagogically significant, a moment of fusion between the received horizons of our traditions and the omnipresent possibility of experiential insight (Gadamer, 2013, p. 317); to be drawn forth into a sense of indebtedness to our relational co-existence (Jardine, 1998, p. 71); to be pierced by a shaft of light, emanating, it seems, like a red lantern from *this* vibrant maple leaf before us (Zwicky, 2003, p. L53).

The ecohermeneutically minded teacher works to clear the "free space" (Jardine, 2012) for a "serendipitous turn" of attention and, suddenly and unexpectedly, perchance, *everything* echoes through the emptiness like the sound of wind through leaves. For a fleeting moment, all that is rigid and certain melts away, and there is only the fermenting, earthy-sweet smell of decay and wonder. "What kind of mushrooms are these?" The question hangs. Not yours, a world's.

> Wittgenstein: 174. *What is strange is really the surprise; the question "How is it possible!"* (1982)

ৱ

Given the full application of attention to an object, teachable moments can quickly proliferate beyond the pale of prescribed learning objectives and timetables. "Why have those leaves turned red?" The managerial mind recoils and yearns for rule and control: "Class, when I ring the bell, everyone will line up and be quiet. It is simple chemistry really, winter is approaching and the tree has begun suspending its production of chlorophyll." But this quick answer is, as environmental theorist Neil Evernden has noted, the "how" not the "why" (1993, p. 18). This response—if it is the only one allowed to be voiced—and its passive parody on the test does not demonstrate *understanding*, rather it demonstrates the authority of the teacher and the "sciences"[2] to reify the abstract qualities of leaves in general and provide definitive explanations. It

---

2   Here "sciences" refers to an image of science as a kind of thinking constrained by rigid and simplistic canons of logic idealized in the mid-seventeenth century by thinkers like Francis Bacon. Ecohermeneutics rejects a hard and fast dichotomy between "scientific thought" and the kinds of thinking that we more commonly associate with philosophy, poetry, and the arts. For a related discussion on the false dichotomy between reason and imagination within an educational context see Egan, 1997.

jumps quickly back from the phenomenological edge to more certain ground, withdrawing as it were, from the question, the object, the possibility of thinking intensely and beautifully together.

> We desensitize, we abstract, and we fragment the leaf and student. The leaf is examined as separate from the tree, chlorophyll as separate from the sun, and all these scraps of knowledge as separate from context and place. In addition each fragment is parsed into a disciplinary box—the leaf in biology, chlorophyll in chemistry, the sun in astronomy. It is not unusual to encounter this kind of fragmentation throughout education, bits and pieces that can be gathered and that might, if we are lucky, fit together in a more cogent whole. (Creeping Snowberry & Blenkinsop, 2010, p. 55)

But what could a fistful of red leaves possibly *mean*? Ecohermeneutics does not seek to reject the kinds of analytical thinking we generally associate with the empirical sciences in favour of the explanatory power of more poetic tropes or something of the like. The tree *is* suspending its production of chlorophyll (at least, that is one way of looking at it). Rather it seeks to decompose the univocal character of essentialist discourses that derive authority not from some privileged access to reality or empirical discipline to "capture" phenomena accurately, but from cultural-historical power relations and circumstance. But before we critically analyze the manifold ways in which the dominant culture seeks to sever us from sensuous and multivocal experience of, say, a fistful of red leaves (vis-à-vis disciplinary fragmentation, abstraction, desacralization, etc.), let's stay on the phenomenological edge for a moment longer.

Here, the ecohermeneutic educator shares something of the essence of a nature poet as poet and philosopher Jan Zwicky has described it: "The essence is a commitment to acknowledging, mourning, and celebrating *what-is*—its non-, its extra-, and its fully human dimensions" (2008, p. 86). The disposition of this sense of "lyric realism" rejects reductive explanations that attempt to straightforwardly capture the complexity, polyphony and ineffability of what-is into human constructs. The fundamental gesture of lyric thinking is rather a disciplined act of attending with the understanding that things beyond the human can be "every bit as ontologically robust" (p. 86). This is, as poet Gary Snyder has called it, the "real work" of the poet and, as I would like to suggest, the vocation of the educator in a time of ecological emergency.

> The real work is what we really do. And what our lives really are. And if we can live the work we have to do, knowing that we are real, and that the world is real, then it becomes right. And that's the real work: to make the world as real as it is and to find ourselves as real as we are within it. (1980, p. 82)

In a similar vein, philosopher, poet and typographer Robert Bringhurst adds:

> What does poetry say? It says that what-is is: that the real is real, and that it is alive. It speaks the grammar of being. It sings the polyphonic structure of meaning itself...
>   Poetry is the language of being: the breath, the voice, the song, the speech of being. It does not need us. We are the ones in need of it. If we haven't learned to hear it, we will also never speak it. (2006, p. 43)

A pedagogy informed by ecohermeneutic imagination suggests that if someone makes a free space for remaining on the phenomenological edge with things—to learn how to hear the language of being—and to reflect on interrelatedness *seriously* (this is not to say without play or humour), perhaps we may more readily recognize a fistful of red maple leaves as part of a real, agential world with intrinsic value, teachings and perspective beyond the horizon of human. If "thinking ecologically" in education comprised the development of disciplines and practices of attending to the world and reflecting upon its forms—similar to those of the nature poet—perhaps we might more readily recognize the sound of wind in the leaves as a meaningful gesture that we can think *with*? As Zwicky illustrates in this selection from her poem, "The Geology of Norway": When we think intensely and beautifully, something happens.

The sound of wind in leaves,
that was what puzzled me, it took me years
to understand that it was music.
Into silence, a gesture.
A sentence: that it speaks.
This is the mystery: meaning.
Not that these folds of rock exist
but that their beauty, here,
now, nails us to the sky.
(1998, p. 34)

Momentarily emptied of our our-centeredness, stopped in our tracks, something addresses us from beyond our wanting and doing, beyond our constructs (and not without imaginative encirclement): the faerie-flecked cap of an agaric, faces in the grains of a wooden desk, a sonorous refrain in the wind—rich with meaning. For those in the business of words—poets, writers, but also teachers of all disciplines—it is not always clear how to share or debrief the significance of being addressed from "out there" beyond our comfortable constructs.

Chapter One

Zwicky (2012) has argued that at least some experiences of the (natural) world are genuinely ineffable: in particular what she calls the world's "resonant structures," which are difficult to parse into straightforward prose and analytic logic. If this is so—and if those structures are important because they are also where meaning resides—then how might we foster awareness of resonance? Admittedly poets have better established traditions and practices of attending to resonant structures and are granted the cultural space and license to experiment with form, prosody, metaphor and other devices to respond to the resonant features or aspects of the world. The logic of "good poetry" [3] (and good dance, and visual art and the arts in general) *is* resonant, which is why, of course, good art does a better job at getting it right about the resonant aspects of things. In education, however, we seem to lack the very words, not to mention the cultural precedent, for reflecting seriously upon both genuinely ineffable experiences and those that elicit us from beyond the wanting and doing of our present cultural-historical horizon.

Despite the surprise each time we hear the question properly—*how is it possible!*—standing serendipitously on the edge of a vast cerulean sky or nailed to it by some resonant gesture, this is the mystery: meaning.

> To me it is clear that things have meaning because they *are* meaning, and that language has meaning—or *can* have meaning—because it can speak, poorly but truly, of some of the things that language is not...
>
> Language listens to the world. I listen with it. What I hear when I listen is a question, which is listening itself. The question often changes form: from silence to breathing to speaking to music to voices to visions to silence again. (Bringhurst, 2006, pp. 62–63)

"Why have those leaves turned red?" The question hangs. Well, let's go have a look at this tree. What might the tree be communicating with these red, lantern-like leaves? What do the falling leaves sound like? What does it mean? When I ring the bell, I invite everyone to listen.

---

3   I use the seemingly contentious term "good poetry" here as Zwicky defines it: "Good poetry, like all meaningful thought, traces a gesture of address. It enacts ontological attention. Metaphor is one of the means it uses to do this" (2003, p. 158). In a similar sense, we might think of "good curriculum" as a kind of "ontological signpost" (Zwicky, 2008, p. 88) pointing towards the world; metaphor is one of the means it uses to do this (a topic further discussed in chapter four).

> The sound of wind in the leaves.
> Ah, music.

༄

On the way to work she passes shopping malls, factories, office buildings, schools, the staggering hubbub of *human* heaped upon everything *else*. She feels troubled by the geometry of things, by the very architectonics of her daily life. All about her the environment insists, *it has always been this way*, but she knows there has always been something *else* as well. Not something beyond, not the transcendental cul-de-sac of Heaven or the high-rimmed Republic of Forms, but something vibrant and alive *beneath* all this. Something *within* the world, *in-between* things that speaks to her sometimes. And though she yearns to share her affinities

> *it is difficult to explain.*

Now she stands in front of her class, reaching for this ineffable sense of kinship with things, pointing and hoping, not for explanations, but for the right kinds of questions, for what presses questions upon us. Exasperated by the humdrum volume of prescribed outcomes, the ubiquitous din of the air-conditioner, she cries out the unthinkable—

> Pay *attention!*

> No, not to the finger, to *this*.
> *H*ere.

All the other advantages of instruction are without interest.

༄

The philosophy of education at the root of ecohermeneutics is the sense that there is a kind of wisdom, or, at least, a clearing for wisdom to germinate in the act of fixing our attention on something *real*; or put in slightly different terms, on something *relational*, something *ecological*. This is by no means an original contribution and something the hermeneutic tradition shares with a diverse array of folk, contemplative and wisdom traditions from presocratic Greek philosophy (Zwicky, 1995, 2003; Bringhurst, 2002), to "erotic" manifestations of

Christianity and Western intellectualism (Lilburn, 2008a), to Buddhist-inspired pedagogical practices (Seidel & Jardine, 2014) and Indigenous epistemologies of place (Sheridan & Longboat, 2006). In this sense, an *ecohermeneutic pedagogy* serves only as a "traditional" reminder—as in the ringing of a bell—that although bureaucratized learning systems dominate, and neoliberal tropes trickle down the pyramid like tarsand, and one is forced to choose between shallow psychological discourses to explain the crisis in adolescence and shallow climate change discourses to explain the ecological crisis...*ding!*)))

> [A]ll that confronts us is the world, gesturing at us. The world has patterns, of which our thinking is part. It makes us feel good to experience these patterns: it is one way of coming home. (Zwicky, 2003, p. L14).

Education as home-coming, as home making (literally *ecopoïesis*),[4] as finding ourselves already home in a world thrumming with resonant meaning. Then, the question is only: are you going to take part, and if so, how?

What if, instead of inculcating the virtues of energy-saving lightbulbs and composting (not that there is anything wrong with that, some of my best friends compost), we approached ecological education as a practice of learning to fix our attention on the resonant structures of meaning—the *voice*—of the world? Might we begin to recognize with more frequency the immeasurable, yet strangely familiar, polyphony of things? And if so, would the rest follow of itself? If we acknowledged that *this* tree really exists as much as we do, could we continue to exploit the forests so callously? Modern Western schooling produces many educated people adept at reading texts and reading the world through or as texts, but these proficiencies come too often with the leviathanic ethos of Eurocentrism; or if nominally "anti-imperial," they maintain the colonial logic of anthropocentric hubris. If one is to take ecologically minded critiques of anthropocentrism (Lewis & Kahn, 2010), dualism (Plumwood, 1993) and

---

4   Zwicky clearly distinguishes between finding oneself at home and trying to make oneself at home, claiming that, "To the extent that one must try to make oneself at home in the world, to that extent one is not part of the ecology of what-is" (2003, p. L28). While this rings true, I want to push back against the anthropic monopoly on the agency of the verb 'making' by pointing to its etymological origins in the Old English *macian* and German *makon*, which can both be translated as 'to fit.' This image implies a more reciprocal and dialogical relationship with the world, or as Zwicky has described, "the fit of response and co-response" with the ecology of what-is (p. L27). That said, *ecopoïesis* does not try to force a fit with heavy handed, abstract axioms like "everything is connected" or "think global, act local" but entails a disciplined act of listening in order to elicit ontological attention.

univocal empiricism (Jardine, 1998) seriously, educational research and praxis must recognize the pedagogical significance of making space for more-than-human alterity and voice (Fawcett, 2000; McKenzie, 2005; Russell, 2005; Bai, 2009; Rautio, 2013). What's more, place-based education projects informed by critical ecohermeneutic thinking in colonial states such as Canada must attempt to thoughtfully, humbly and ethically weave with decolonial pedagogies aimed at the revitalization of Indigenous lands and life (Tuck & Wang, 2012; see also Battiste, 2013; Chambers, 1999; Donald, 2009; Four Arrows, 2013). If construing mind, language and imagination without sourcing its ecological origins extends anthropocentrism, and by extension colonial interests, as Joe Sheridan and Dan Roronhiake:wen Longboat (2006) have claimed, the recognition of more-than-human meaning must comprise a key component of decolonial pedagogies (these themes will be revisited in chapter four and chapter nine).

The hermeneutic tradition calls upon educators in a time of ecological emergency to not only impart the rhetoric of sustainability but to find ways to both read and be read by the world. Such an "ecopoetic turn" (chapter three) comprises a means for modern Western thought to begin to move beyond a use-relation with "natural resources" towards resonance with the interrelated ecology of a more-than-human world. As Bringhurst has written:

> Reading, for me, is the proof of being at home: a quintessential part of the equation that enables us to reach across the fence between the world and ourselves without destroying what we find. The most basic parts of that equation, surely, are eating and being eaten. Can't have one without the other. May not seem so in the restaurant or the bookstore, but walking in the forest or sitting by the stream, we know it works both ways: being fed and feeding, reading and being read. (2006, p. 9)

To read and be read: ecological literacy as knowing it works both ways.

ॐ

There is a troubling tendency in the dominant culture to think of language as nothing more than the capacity to acquire and employ a system of communication to express human subjectivity (well, sometimes we also grant computers the capacity for "language," but almost never animals,[5] and certainly not fungi or maple trees). Critically speaking, one of the primary tasks of ecohermeneutic

---

5   For a fascinating account of how animals are being "erased from our consciousness" and the many ways in which language affects our relationships with animals and the natural world, see ecolinguist Arran Stibbe's *Animals Erased* (2012).

inquiry is to engender a kind of ecocritical discourse analysis in education in order to bring greater awareness to the linguistic dimension of the ecological crisis (Bowers, 1993; Harre, Brockmeier & Mühlhäuser, 1999); a theme that will be addressed throughout this book. But if an ecohermeneutic approach to pedagogy also seeks to develop the capacity to read place and be read by place— or put in different terms, to develop the deep relational ontologics required to acknowledge "place as a co-teacher" (Blenkinsop & Beeman, 2010; Blenkinsop & Piersol, 2013)–it will invariably confront the more fundamental problem of what comprises *language*?[6] And, a related, but different concern: how the more-than-human means?

While an in-depth account of "linguistic ecology" is beyond the scope of this book, it should be noted that critical ecohermeneutics, as I envision it, both provides philosophical support for and draws inspiration from the work of those scholars engaged with the ecological turn in linguistics (Fill & Mühlhäusler, 2001; Goatly, 2000; Bowers, 2009; Stibbe, 2012; Steffensen & Fill, 2014).[7] Clearly a new paradigm of linguistic research that takes into account not only the social contexts in which languages are embedded but also the complex relationship between language and ecology provides a corrective measure to the anthropocentric echo chamber of conventional linguistics. That said, the work of Danish ecolinguists Jorgen Christian Bang and Jorgen Door (2007), for example, which is concerned with the development of situational dialogue models, semantic matrixes and models for analyzing deictic phenomena (*deixis* is used in linguistics to subsume those features of language which refer directly to the personal, temporal or locational characteristics of the situation within which an utterance takes place—an ecolinguistic approach claims language cannot be understood unless understood in dialectical relationship with the environment), while fascinating, can strike the educationist and the non-linguist as a little *applied*. It is also not clear how or if the "dialectical philosophy" that informs

---

6   See *The Language Myth* (1981) by Roy Harris and a collection of essays titled *Redefining Linguistics* (1990) edited by Hayley Davis and Talbot Taylor for examples of some of the challenges involved in defining what "language" is and the implications for determining the subject matter of linguistics.

7   Although linguists such as Edward Sapir have been writing about the relationship between language and environment as early as 1912, it was not until the 1990s that all the different approaches which in some way link the study of language with ecology were brought together, and a unified—though still diverse—branch of linguistics was established, which is called ecolinguistics (see Fill & Mühlhäusler, 2001 for a collection of some of the most important contributions to the field; see Bang & Door, 2007 for an example of applied ecolinguistics; also Lechevrel, 2009 for a history of ecological approaches to language).

their work (keeping in mind that philosophical positions in the field are as diverse as its proponents) is "consonant" with ecohermeneutics in interpreting the (pedagogic) significance of particular more-than-human beings.

By way of a quick illustration, the following passage provides a sample of the kind of language (and ontological presuppositions) employed by a dialectical approach:

> Dialectical philosophy does not consider the universe as based on "dead matter" or elementary particles without history. This is a kind of reductionism. It does not work from a dualism between mind and matter (mind and brain) or organic and inorganic. On the contrary, our dialectical theory views the universe as an inter-connected, communicating whole and a complex system with emergent properties. Like deep ecology and other holistic approaches, dialectical theory views the universe as inherently and innately divine. An implication of such a paradigm shift is that the relational concept *communication* and *energy* takes the position formerly held by *elementary particle* and *mass*. Communication always resonates at every level and dimension of reality: if a person eats some food and a metabolic process takes place, then the food—and the metabolic communication between the food and the body—vibrates in the body, in the social relationships and in the mental dimension. (Bang & Door, 2007, p. 55)

While the holistic undertones of this ecological turn in dialectical philosophy are compelling, there remains, for me, a troubling potential for attenuating the phenomenology of particular things and our relational responsibilities in the "rush" to an inter-connected whole. Granted a certain amount of reduction in particularity may be inevitable when trying to name, describe and deal with vast, complex categories like "nature" or "the world" or "the universe" in scientific ways, but the work of ecohermeneutics, at the level of education at least, is to imploy[8] an ecological understanding of language to return us to the sensuous and imaginative resonance between experience and things as they are lived.

For example, although Zwicky (1992, 2003) has an ongoing interest in the significance of geometric thinking and mathematical proofs as a form of seeing-as (ostensibly the "opposite" of a sensuous, phenomenological description), she has warned against "ecological" kinds of thinking that standardize particularity, maintaining that nature is not merely a collection of "undomesticated biomass" (or, by extension, dimensionless "energy").

---

8   I will use the archaic verb "imploy" here to both avoid the exploitative associations of its modern relative 'employ' and to harken back to its Latin root *implicari*, "to be involved in or attached to." In the 16th and 17th century the word also had the senses "enfold, entangle and imply" deriving directly from the Latin and also forming the root of the word *implicate*.

> If we think of nature as ecology, its "individuals" are really nothing more than nodes in a huge network—imagine the mathematical points of intersection that define a geodesic dome. Remove any of these nodes, or pull it out of place, and everything else in the system shifts to accommodate the change. A remarkable interdependence. But the odd thing is, as the analogy with mathematical points makes clear, it leaves the individuals—the mountains, the rivers, the swallows and frogs—ontologically dimensionless. Once again they turn out to be nothing more than *sets of relata*. But what we love when we love a mountain, or a river, or an animal, is nothing so abstract, much less it is a whole system that, in a sense, expresses itself as a series of relations that define a given node. (Zwicky, 2008, p. 90)

So while a geodesic dome provides an intriguing and fitting image to think through interrelatedness, and while the interaction between food and body as a kind of "communication" is a fascinating topic for linguistics to contend with, ecohermeneutics is more concerned with how to imploy language to draw one towards attentive consideration of a particular mountain, that frog there, that emerald green one with the conspicuous dark stripe through its eye, *this* tree (within which, of course, *everything* resonates).

ৡ

Ecological linguistics for Bringhurst—for whom linguistics is a "branch of natural history"—means coming to understand language as a continuum that includes "everything from birdsong to linear algebra and symbolic logic" and most of that continuum, or all of it, "is occupied with stories" (2006, p. 167). The task of an ecological approach to linguistics, and as I contend for ecohermeneutic pedagogy, is thus less concerned with developing models for analyzing deictic phenomena or with repurposing scientific nomenclature to bolster holistic paradigms (both, however, eminently worthwhile endeavours), and is more concerned with keeping language connected to life "in the wild."

> For a language, life "in the wild" means life as a functioning part of a cultural ecosystem, where chatter, laughter, conversations, stories, songs, and dreams are as continuous as breathing.... Life in the wild, for a language as for any living entity—animal, plant, fungus, protozoan, or bacterium—means a dependable and nourishing interconnection with the rest of life on the planet...
>
> Its speakers are in a sense the lungs of the language. Without them it will neither speak nor breathe. But without that other nourishing attachment—not to its speakers but to the world that surrounds them—the ability to speak would be of little value. A language severed from the world might go on talking, but the memory of its referents

would fade, and its standards of truth and beauty would wither. After a time we would find it had nothing of substance to say. (2006, pp. 160–161)

Ecohermeneutics means imploying language and attentive disciplines in education to remediate our "hyperseparation" (Plumwood, 2002) from nourishing interconnections with the rest of life on the planet. As Jardine has claimed, the disciplines of school not only undergo but require constant renewal and transformation in order to remain substantive and healthy (or to put it unfashionably, to remain connected to standards of truth and beauty). This is what it means to envisage education as "part and parcel of the breath of the world" (1998, p. 3).

The "ecological turn" has spawned a diverse array of emerging fields in the last several decades: ecopedagogy, ecophenomenology, ecofeminism, political ecology, environmental history, integral ecology, ecosemiotics, ecocriticism, and ecopoetics, just to name a few. While the connections and contentions between fields is interesting and important work, perhaps the most judicious thing to say about ecolinguistics and ecohermeneutics at this time is that they are related among the emerging kith of ecocritical fields. According to Arran Stibbe on the on-line *Language and Ecology Research Forum*, ecolinguistic research ranges from "the impact of advertising discourse in encouraging ecologically damaging consumption to the power of nature poetry to encourage respect for the natural world" (n.d.). Ecohermeneutics shares in these interests, however, its pedagogical objectives run deeper than exploring the power of nature poetry. It is concerned rather with how education can co-create free spaces for "ecopoetic encounter" with more-than-human alterity and return human thinking into resonance with the wisdom and humility of "ecology" (here I mean ecology literally, as in study of the *oikos*). Obviously an ecological understanding of language is a key component, but when meaning goes more-than-human we discover quickly that we tend to slip continuously between voice and silence, responding and listening, the business of words and the vocation of learning. How, then, might we imploy language to listen to the world? Or, to pose the question in more practical terms for educators: What do people say when they are conversing with the world? Well, put simply: "They sing songs and tell stories. They make poems in other words: lyric poems and narrative poems. And wherever there is a language, that is what happens" (Bringhurst, 2006, p. 163). Education as storytelling: where chatter, laughter, conversations, stories, songs and dreams are as continuous as breathing.

Chapter One

ক

Something wonderful has happened.
Clumsy yellow rain boots slow her mad rush home, considerably.
She is stalled again by mother's doubt & incessant vacuuming.
Finally, they are on their way back   to investigate.
She had discovered it earlier that morning in the schoolyard.
A giant ring of mushrooms, a perfect circle of magic.
A bell rang & she ran home.

She knows something has happened.
Before she sees the slow crimson machine advancing, relentlessly.
She is struck again by mother's composure & incessant decorum.
Mr. Bacon, the groundskeeper   cuts perfect lines.
Waving back from his brand new streamlined riding mower.
The field is immaculate & without enchantment.
The school bell rings.

ক

What does it mean to return education towards the nourishing interconnections of earthly life? How does one prepare for "co-creating the possibility for ecopoetic encounter"? What does it mean to teach with a commitment to acknowledging, mourning, and celebrating *what-is*—its non-, its extra-, and its fully human dimensions? Zwicky (2003) has suggested, "ontological understanding is rooted in the perception of patterned resonance in the world," and that, "Philosophy, practiced as a setting of things side by side until the similarity dawns, is a form of ontological appreciation" (p. L7). Ecohermeneutics is, in essence, also committed to ontological appreciation and returning education towards the significance of "ecological being" (i.e., interbeing) and the ethical ramifications thereof. It too is rooted in attentive perception of the pattern of what-is in order to recognize the significance of interrelatedness, to take it *seriously*. As Bringhurst has explained, "...the life of the mind, like the life of the forest, only exists in an interactive and polymorphous form. Your life may be yours alone, but unless a lot of other things are living, neither am I and neither are you. This is true for the individual, true for the species, and true for the mind" (2006, p. 67). These ecologically sage observations are, in essence, a trace of the kind of ontological insight that ecohermeneutics aims to elicit in educational experiences. Notwithstanding the importance of learning about recycling, ecological footprint, or biodiversity, an ecohermeneutic pedagogy also works to clear space for the recognition that we are co-constituted by the world all the way down.

As a practice, it might be thought of as the disciplined training of the attention to recognize (i.e., to re-think, to think again and again, to recycle) particular things as immanent interpenetrating structures and processes. *Everything* is ontologically robust. To keep our thinking fluid by breaking out beyond the confines of a narrowly conceived ontology premised solely on anthropic agency into the pitter-patter of a living earthen interbeing of which the disciplines of schooling are a part, not an exception (Jardine, 1998). Or, in another sense, it is something like *attuning* thinking to the polyphony of interbeing, and joining in, rather than drowning out. I want to say ecohermeneutic insight is something like the experience of making a connection, like astonishment at the now self-evident. But really, the connections already exist. As Jardine reminds us, "We are *already* connected to the Earth, to each other, to our children, albeit in ambiguous and multivocal ways" (1998, p. 22). Similarly, in his overview of hermeneutics and education, philosopher Shaun Gallagher has claimed: "The living human being understands the world as he finds himself already in it, not as an anaemic egological entity eruditely confronting an opposing objective entity. Interpretation is not something that I (the epistemological ego) do, but something that I am involved in" (1992, p. 45).

What-is already means. We are already running with it.

ॐ

Here. Two things I found for you, set side by side:

Czech poet, dissident and politician Vaclav Havel (as cited in Capra, 2002, introduction):

> Education is the ability to perceive the hidden connections between phenomena.

And mycologist Paul Stamets (2005, p. 125):

> Mycelium is, in essence, a digestive cellular membrane, a fusion between a stomach and a brain, a nutritional and informational sharing network. It is an archetype of matter

and life: our universe is based upon these networking structures. Your job is to become embedded into the mind-set of this matrix and use its connections for running with mycelium.

Zwicky continues: "A metaphor sets one thing beside another and says, 'See, they have the same form'. Which is to say: they make the same gesture; they mean in the same way" (2003, p. L8).

chapter two

mycelia & the hermeneutics beneath us

> Beings eat one another. This is the fundamental business of the world. It is the whole, not any of its parts, that must prevail, and this whole is always changing. There is no indispensable species, and no indispensable culture. Especially not a culture that dreams of eating without being eaten, and that offers the gods not even the guts or the crumbs. (Bringhurst, 2006, p. 44)

Consider what mycelia mean. An interwoven matrix of branching, thread-like hyphae that course and ramify throughout most ecosystems, symbiotically facilitating nutrient uptake, decomposing organic matter, remediating toxic accumulations in the soil, and generating ever-thickening layers of fecund humus (Stamets, 2005). Despite their keystone role in maintaining the health and function of ecosystems, these beings perform primarily beneath our everyday awareness, and most folk remain oblivious to the existence and life-sustaining significance of mycelia. Occasionally, we may happen upon the fruiting bodies of this living, subterranean entanglement (if we live, or make time to go, or are taken to the places where fungi still bloom, and if we pay attention) and only then do we become aware of the vibrant webwork beneath us and, perhaps, if our earthly connection has not been severed or schooled out of us, we are reminded of the interdependent ethos of a "humus-filled" existence.[1]

---

[1] Jardine has noted the importance of a humus-filled life and the way we are living out our disconnectedness and disengagement in educational theory and practice in often unnoticeable and unvoiced ways. "As we sever our connections with the Earth, it ceases to be

Chapter Two

Mushrooms, depending on the species, have traditionally been accorded magical, mystical and exalted significance in folk traditions and spiritual practices in myriad cultures around the world (Tupper, 2002; Morgan, 1995; Schultes & Hofmann, 1987). In the modern Western world, by and large, the spell and cultural import of mushrooms has been replaced with generalized suspicion of these strange and potentially poisonous (or mind-altering) beings outside of special interest groups. This seems particularly true of the "wild" varieties. The white button mushrooms we are accustomed to encountering in grocery stores are comfortably cultivated, labeled, and sanitized, but in the wilderness, only a scattering of mushroom species have been identified[2] and they can teem in an unnerving proliferation of form and composition. "What kind of mushrooms are these?" Teacher begrudgingly admits: "I am not sure, but they might be poisonous. Let's head back." At the end of the day, most folk never get a chance to encounter mushrooms amongst the lush, verdant floors of a boreal forest just after an early autumn shower, let alone the resonant mycelia that (in)form them from beneath. The identity of mycelia and meaning has been severed.

ৡ

Now consider knowledge as an interwoven mass of branching, thread-like networks that course and ramify predominantly beneath our everyday awareness. Fruiting bodies of thought emerge from the cultural-historical humus of a particular place and—in healthy ecocultural systems and intellectual landscapes—bloom, grow, spore and convey something of the world before decaying and putrefying as all things must. In this way, we may come to tentatively know (some) things as embedded in living and impermanent processes that evolve and require constant and generative reinterpretation. The inevitable decay of bodies and knowing is not something that need be mourned or prolonged, but rather revitalized by new generations and forms of life that—with a little good

---

 our abode and becomes a meaningless objective mechanism which is at the disposal of our whim and consumptive fantasies. And, correlatively, as the Earth loses its humus, its living, generative character, the subject loses its humanity by losing the connectedness with the humus out of which it has emerged" (1998, pp. 9-10).

2 According to Stamets (2005) the fungi kingdom is populated with between 1 to 2 million species. "Fungi outnumber plants at a ratio of at least 6 to 1. About 10 percent of fungi are what we call mushrooms, and only about 10 percent of the mushroom species have been identified, meaning that our taxonomic knowledge of mushrooms is exceeded by our ignorance by at least one order of magnitude. The surprising diversity of fungi speaks to the complexity needed for a healthy environment" (pp. 10-11).

teaching and humility—remain attuned to the places that shape, sustain and calibrate knowing. Viewed in this way, the vocation of the educator is to keep the disciplines of knowing connected to the world as it is lived; to keep open the possibility of ramifying the mycelial-like growth of knowledge by tending to the generativity of the soils in which it thrives (which includes mycoremediating it from latent *epistemicides* [Paraskeva, 2011; K. Bennett, 2007] and other hypostatized elements).

This is, in essence, what Hannah Arendt referred to as the basis of intergenerational learning: "The basic fact of education is natality: the fact that children are born into the world" (1969, p. 174). Or as Jardine, drawing on German philosopher Hans-Georg Gadamer, has maintained, we must accept a fundamentally hermeneutic reality:

> The places we venture with (or without) [our students] in (and out of) school—spelling, reading mathematics, poetry, art, biology, chemistry, philosophy, Dutch Calvinism, Impressionism, writing, hermeneutics, ecology, and so on—are continuously becoming constituted and understood and inhabited differently. They are, so to speak *living* places or spaces or rooms, (or, if you will, "living disciplines") that form part of our living Earthly inheritance, and as such—as *living*, that is, as susceptible to the future—we "must accept the fact that future generations will understand differently" (Gadamer, 1989, p. 340). (Jardine, 2012, p. 152)

Regrettably, many once "reasonable" bodies of knowledge have been hypostatized as privileged epistemic foundations—methodically decontextualized and denatured (Plumwood, 2002)—and thus severed from both our phenomenological experience of the world and the lived problems of the present day. Modernity has, by and large, failed to recognize[3] that severing knowing from the generative, interpretive and vernacular matrix of understanding that

---

3   The calcification of epistemology is, in fact, defined by its lack of *re-cognition*, its inability or unwillingness to *re-think* or *recycle*. As Zwicky (2003) has written, this phenomenon of seeing again or seeing differently—or as Wittgenstein called it "seeing-as"—is crucial to the mystery of meaning. "The moment of recognition happens as if by magic; and yet, when we reflect on it, we see—its very name tells us this—that it is impossible without prior experience. What becomes puzzling then is the phenomenon of insight, the creation (apparently) of new meaning. Here, we forget that to recognize can mean to re-think, as in *think through differently*. It need not always signify mere repetition of a former cognition. We say in such cases not only that we recognize X (as Y) but that we realize X *is* Y.... That is, 'recognition', even in apparently straightforward cases, involves re-organization of experience—an act of contextualization, a sensing of connexions between aspects of immediate experience and other experiences" (p. L1).

informs humus-filled ways of being-in-the-world does not bring us nearer to some essential kernel of universal truth. Rather, the historical distortion of reason combined with aggressive colonial fantasies has led to learning as an ossified tautology of dominion and self-interest—a curriculum of extinction based on the rote repetition of archaic values. As D. Smith (1999) has written, the appeal of the hermeneutic imagination resides, in part, in the general state of exhaustion of what philosopher Karl-Otto Apel has called the "dogmatic-normative" traditions of epistemology and metaphysics as they functioned foundationally in the establishment and continuation of contemporary discourse domains from the Enlightenment to the present. The exhaustion of Western forms of discourse is due to a "crisis of value...that cannot be resolved simply by appealing to traditional forms of logic and authority" (p. 28).

Ontological hypostatization impoverishes the humus of being; leaching its poetic (as in *making*) fecundity, desecrating its cultural-historical composition, and calcifying knowing into rigid, unimaginative and univocal certainties that lack calibrated resonance with the temporal ecology of what-is. In effect, we become dulled to the polyphony of interbeing, unable to attune to the thinking of things, or, as Bringhurst has succinctly described it, unable to recognize the identity of poetry and thinking (2006, p. 139). We become obdurate and, to a certain extent, suspicious of our own lived experience *and* the lived experience of "others" (ancestral, subaltern, more-than-human, etc.); more ready to accept the leviathanic dictates of everyday certainties and common-sense inevitabilities. Ultimately, even when faced with the ecocidal despoilment of our home, we lose the ability to hear "simpleminded" observations that ring true.

> I hold the very simpleminded view that everything is related to everything else—and that every one is related to everyone else, and that every species is related to every other. The only way out of this tissue of interrelations, it seems to me, is to stop paying attention, and to substitute something else—hallucination, greed, pride, or hatred, for example—for sensuous connection to the facts. I think it is not the world's task to entertain us, but ours to take an interest in the world.
>
> I also subscribe to the view—not original with me—that the world is constructed in such a way as to be as interesting as possible. This is a deep tautology. Our minds, our brains, our hearts are grown out of the world, just as buttercups and mushrooms are. The world is us, and we are little replicas and pieces of the world. How could the world be anything other than as interesting as possible to us?
>
> Yet all it takes to break that link is to try to control the world, or take it for granted, or ask it not to change or not to complain while we continue to carve it up. All it takes—and this is not, evidently, very difficult to do—is to sever the identity of poetry and thinking. (Bringhurst, 2006, pp. 157-158)

ঀ

I like everything about the verb *deliquesce,* as in the mushroom *deliquesced* as it reached maturity, decaying and slowly liquefying as it returns to the dark, moist earth. It provides a fitting image I think to describe the process of critical ecohermeneutic inquiry. I imagine fruiting bodies of knowledge as mushrooms emerging from the mycelial matrix of cultural-historical understandings and developing robust domes and stalks, reproductive spores if the conditions are favourable, but *deliquescing* as they reach maturity, putrefying and decaying back into the earth to reconnect with an evolving planetary ecology. The critical ecohermeneutic imagination thus works to decompose the ecologically destructive elements of epistemic certainty, to *deliquesce* ontological calcifications, to ecocritically recalibrate habitual being-in-the-world. Pedagogically speaking, an ecohermeneutic approach is aimed at learning how to read and be read, eat and be eaten, to know it works both ways.

> Poets are more like mushrooms, or fungus—they can digest the symbol-detritus. (Snyder, 1980, p. 71)

ঀ

When you think intensely and beautifully, something happens. That something is called poetry.
If you think that way and teach at the same time, wisdom gets in your teachings.
If students hear you, it gets in their hearts.
If you think that way and teach with place, then pedagogy resonates with ecology.
But poetry *exists* in any case. The question is only: are you going to take part, and if so, how?

ঀ

Critical ecohermeneutics is a kind of philosophic mycoremediation; a term borrowed from mycologist Paul Stamets (2005) who describes it as a process whereby mycelia are used to inoculate contaminated soils (or other substrates), remove toxins and generate the conditions for flourishing biodiversity. Mycoremediation is a healing process that represents one facet of a broader strategy to improve ecosystem health that Stamets has termed *mycorestoration*.[4] An emphasis on the remedial and generative capacity of the ecohermeneutic imagination is important because we find ourselves already in a fragmented and increasingly toxic wasteland, all too familiar with its economic rationalities, its patriarchal dualities, its forests and children as standing-reserves.

Johnathan Skinner, editor of the publication *ecopoetics*, has also drawn on mycological metaphors, construing interdisciplinary sites of ecological interpretation and writing as "mycoremedial" and suggesting that ecopoetics be conceived as a sort of "mobile contamination unit...cutting across divisions of labour, crossing and acknowledging linguistic, cultural and species borders" (2001, p. 8). Revitalizing the landscape of existential possibility will require interdisciplinary and eco-socio-diverse approaches. Ecohermeneutic inquiry is part of a mycorestorative strategy to accelerate the decomposition of essentialist and anthropocentric toxins, as it prepares fragmented cultural ecosystems for reinhabitation by other ways of knowing from diverse cultures, fields and species; always deliquescing before it fossilizes, recycling and recalibrating by attuning to the living places and fields of relations beneath us.

> Using fungi first in bioremediation sets the course for other players in the biological community to participate in its rehabilitation.... The introduction of a single fungus, for instance oyster mycelium, into a nearly lifeless landscape triggers a cascade of activity by other organisms. (Stamets, 2005, p. 89)

> Education as oyster mycelium, inoculating the inscape.

ৡ

What is the point of thinking analogically about mycelia and human understanding? Or for that matter, thinking analogically about anything at all? We are, after all, in the midst of multiple, interlocking and escalating crises: an ecological crisis, an economic crisis, an educational crisis. Should we not focus our energy on innovative and technical solutions to these real-world problems? How are interpretative disciplines and lyric thinking supposed to help us clean the oceans, or reprimand the financial class for their profligate glut, or, for that matter, assist our students finding meaningful ways to live

---

4   Mycorestoration practices can be implemented in the following ways: mycoremediation, mycofiltration, mycoforestry, mycopesticides. See Stamets (2005, p. 55).

in this world? Obviously a shift in metaphor alone is not going to transform the world, ecocritical and lyric thought must be coupled with sustained and material praxis, but ecohermeneutics does re-emphasize the need for educators to work on the *level of metaphor*. This is important work, real work, like chopping wood, writing haikus or teaching young people that alternate interior angles of a parallelogram are congruent.

Working on the level of metaphor allows us to dig to the mythopoetic roots of the ecological crisis, which is not a crisis based on resource mismanagement or a lack of sustainable technologies, but a cultural crisis based on depleted imagination and distorted relations (Martusewicz, Edmundson & Lupinacci, 2011; Bowers, 1997). In the *Ecopoetry Anthology*, editors Ann Fisher-Wirth and Laura-Gray Street claim they have become convinced "the environmental crisis is made possible by a profound failure of the imagination. What we humans disregard, what we fail to know and grasp, is easy to destroy: a mountaintop, a coral reef, a forest, a human community. Yet poetry returns us in countless ways to the world of our senses" (2013, p. xxvii). Sensuousness and history, soil and politics, poetry and mathematics: the substrates in which the ecohermeneutic imagination thrums.

If we understand ecological emergency as fundamentally a crisis of relation, then we might better understand the pedagogical significance of *ecopoetic thinking*, which is aimed at drawing us into a kind of pivotal affinity with things. This is one of the most distinctive and powerful qualities of lyric thought, and in that regard, ecohermeneutic pedagogy might more accurately be described as the ecopoetics of education (a theme explored in chapter three). In this sense, thinking ecologically does not so much denote thinking *about* organismic relations and trophic levels in an ecosystem, or employing systems thinking and complexity models to solve problems, or even instilling the virtues of environmental stewardship or any of the other hallmarks of "education for sustainability," rather it denotes the attentive discipline of thinking through/with affinities. As poet Charles Simic has claimed: "A poem is a place where affinities are discovered" (as cited in Zwicky, 2003, p. L47). More broadly, it is a discipline of mindbody and a learned ability to see-as. Drawing on the late work of Wittgenstein, Zwicky has explained thus: "Seeing-as is the result of the natural attunement of our capacities for perception to the world. In understanding (in seeing-as, in the experience of meaning) we show human thinking's fit with being" (2003, p. L26). If the exploitative logic of an instrumental relationship with the world is reproduced through denigrating the capacity to see-as in education—severing the experience of meaning with the world or the identity of poetry and thinking—then maintaining and, indeed, remediating the identity of poetry and thinking is an ecological task. Thinking on the level of metaphor is thus one of the fundamental skills required of educators in a time of ecological emergency.

༄

We have come to experience "school life" and learning as fundamentally prosaic; characterized by fragmentation, emotionlessness and exacerbated by the privileging of epistemic foundations such as anthropocentrism, reductionism, linear causality, and dualism. In the chapters that follow, I will attempt to inoculate (environmental) educational theory with the spawn of critical ecohermeneutic thinking to induce mycoremediation of this pivotal social institution, essential for both cultural reproduction and cultural transformation.[5] Recognizing the intimate relationship between education and hermeneutics, and recycling some of the complex aporias they share, lies at the heart of this inquiry. As Gallagher has maintained:

> Reproduction, authority, and conversation; objectivity, distortion, and transformation: these are issues that both hermeneutics and education must deal with. If education involves understanding and interpretation; if formal educational practice is guided by the use of texts and commentary, reading and writing; if linguistic understanding and communication are essential to educational institutions; if educational experience is a temporal process involving fixed expressions of life and the transmission or critique of traditions; if, in effect, education is a human enterprise, then hermeneutics, which claims all of these as its subject matter, holds out the promise of providing a deeper understanding of the educational process. (1992, p. 24)

I share in the idea that the development of (eco)hermeneutic imagination is crucial if we are to reach for *deeper* understanding in education. I also share the idea that the ecological crisis is, essentially, a product of "modernist thinking" (Blenkinsop, 2012) and if there is to be change then it has to be *deep*, seismic change at the cultural level. But this begs the question, what does *deep* mean?

---

5   This is not to claim that the educational system is *necessary* for cultural transformation or even for "education" per se (see Prakash & Esteva, 2008; Rasmussen, 2011); or that education offers us a panacea for confronting the ecological crisis. This is only to acknowledge that it is a key institution in the cultural reproduction of an ecologically destructive worldview and, as such, presents a critical site for inoculation.

After all, hermeneutic inquiry is nothing new, how does an ecohermeneutic approach allow us to see and be *deeper*?

> Lyric thought is a kind of ontological seismic exploration and metaphors are the charges set by the seismic crew. A good metaphor lets us see more deeply than a weak one. (Zwicky, 2003, p. L44)

Boom!

ৡ

Perhaps seismic charges and exploration crews are not the most ecologically appropriate metaphors? Instead, let's envision tiny bell-shaped fungi scattering the forest floor, which can, as I have claimed, elicit attention to the ramifying and living webwork beneath us. I want to consider how ecohermeneutics might also elicit ontological attunement to the resonant, mycelial-like webwork of knowing that reverberates beneath our everyday experiences in education.

Most conventional schools utilize some kind of mechanized bell in order to call students to attention and—in alignment with the cultural values and imperatives of industrialism—order the experience of student life. What if students were provoked to respond to a different kind of bell? A prayer bell of sorts, though not the heavy-handed, ecclesiastical casts we associate with church spires, but something like the experience of a "bell ringing in the empty sky," such as the one heard in a dream by Japanese Zen priest Kyochiku during which he attained a "moist, green, Earthy" enlightenment (Jardine, 1998). An educational experience that rings true, one that resonates with humble gestures towards our earthen existences, one that aims to draw us into both the exquisite solitariness of nature and its vibrant interrelatedness; both the intertwining kinship of things and the uniqueness and utter irreplaceability of every *thing* (p. 88).

> Whereas a church spire inspires me to lift my eyes to the heavens above, entering a tea room inspires in me something different. The entrance to the ceremonial tea room, by the very way it is built, urges me to incline my body and to bow, bringing me closer to the earth whose textured layers of humus allow buds of tea trees to leaf. The savouring of the tea allows me to touch again this earth that cradles and nourishes both my body and soul. During the Tea Ceremony, I come to respect the fullness of silence, and I become aware of how silently I participate in the constituting of the silence. And in that silence, I experience being-one-with-the-earth. (Aoki as cited in Jardine, 1998, p. 85)

Education as tea ceremony has a nice ring, but is not without its practical pedagogical concerns. How, for example, might we intentionally draw students towards the "resonances of earth" in an age of such mass distraction? How might we imploy language and "nature experiences" to engender respect for the fullness of silence (or at least active listening)? How will foregrounding the interpretability of things yield insight into the very tangible, very alarming realities of an escalating ecological crisis? Yes, yes, but for a moment remain on the phenomenological edge of the gesture, by the way the ceremony is "made," by the co-creation of the possibility for an experience of encounter with the earth—rich with meaning.

In the chapters to come (chapters five through seven) I will attempt to address some of these concerns by means of an "ecohermeneutic inoculation" of some of the key thinkers and concepts of philosophical hermeneutics. While this tradition offers us a uniquely fecund and open field to think through some of these inquires, it is not without its own hypostatizations and epistemicides. This initial mycoremediation process will, I hope, allow us to open the landscape of possibility and consider an ecohermeneutic approach to education in colonial states such as Canada as a kind of place-based process of "re-indigenization" (Kulnieks, Longboat & Young, 2010). But for now I would like to further explore ecohermeneutic inquiry as a kind of *ecopoïesis* or *ecopoetic thinking* (chapters three and four). This will take us deeper into a discussion of the significance of metaphoric thought for if we are to approach pedagogy as a way of inspiring reflection upon the textured layers of humus that inform earthly ways of living, we must dig deep to the mythopoetic roots:

> the mycelia of being.

chapter three

the ecopoetics of education

It starts with rhythm, that much I know. I mean the way the poem moves in time—its pace and gait and proportions. A poem can unfold with the shapely aplomb of a gavotte, or meander, or move with a quicksilver stutter and glide. Each rhythm shapes the energy flow with a distinct logic; each parses the world with a syntax of its own. A poem thinks by the way it moves.

But that raises another question, for rhythmic logic is not conceptual. How can you translate its native terms into categories your mind can deal with? How do you talk about moves your body grasps in a flash? (Lee, 2002, pp. 19-20)

A poem thinks by the way it moves. It conveys meaning by the way it unfolds and approaches, by the way it dances a rhythmic logic on the page, by its very form of being (or, we might say, by the way it imaginatively mimics the gestures of being beneath the words). One is tempted to say all writing thinks by the way it moves (this includes, of course, all the dimensions of experience that can be methodically omitted, flattened, reified). Academic papers also convey meaning, in part, by the way in which they parse experience with a paradigmatic logic; as do love letters, analytical essays and preposterous books on educational philosophy and fungi. This is not to claim these things think in similar ways, on the contrary, their diverse compositions speak to different styles of knowing enacted through form and address (amongst other explicit and tacit qualities of communication). What they are able to enact, that is, as limited as language is, in as much as language can re-create the meaning of something it is not. The rest is left to interpretation; the living hermeneutic whirligig in-between.

What then, as poet and philosopher Tim Lilburn (1995) has asked, does poetry know and how does it know it? Does the world reveal itself differently to poetry than it does to, say, biology or economics, for example? And elsewhere (2008b), underlining the political eros of this line of questioning: what is the most politically efficient use of language? Why do people change? Is being in thrall of beauty, as Lilburn contends, one of the most efficient means of transformation? Ecohermeneutics seeks to bring these inquiries to bear upon education as ecologically significant. If a style of knowing, a culturally privileged and historically wrought methodological approach—like say, instrumental rationality—has fundamentally shaped our relation with the world, and if this humus leaching epistemicide derives its power in part from univocal essentialism, then exploring other ways of looking at things—at the interpretability of world— is an ecological concern.

For the "ecopoetic educator" this entails co-creating a free space to make *radical*[1] pedagogical moves informed by the ecocultural-diverse forms and logics of both human and more-than-human beings. Somewhere "underground" perhaps, just beyond the chain-linked schoolyard fence, somewhere along the sylvan fringe of what is presently thinkable.

> We should have no illusion. Bureaucratized teaching and learning systems dominate the scene, but nevertheless it is everyone's task to find his free space. The task of our human life in general is to find free spaces and learn to move therein. In research this means finding the question, the genuine question. (Gadamer, 1986, p. 59)

In a time of ecological emergency, in the bone-riddled intellectual landscape of modernity where "the ghost of Descartes hovers over the waste dump, the clear cut" (Lilburn, 1995, p. 8), this means *taking up* the hermeneutic task of recognizing what calls for questions and what presses questions upon us. Zwicky: "In fact we are addressed all the time, but we don't always notice this" (2003, p. L52). Here again, it strikes me, the ontological insights native to "good poetry"

---

[1] I use radical here both to convey a commitment to transformative critical pedagogy and also *literally* (which is to say, metaphorically) as ecolinguist Sune Vork Steffensen (2007) has defined it, drawing on its etymology: "The literal meaning of *radical* is that it goes to the *radix*, i.e., the root, of either the problem or the discipline. From these roots it is then possible to develop a true alternative that is not entangled in a development that no matter how promising it was and has been turns out as a literal threat to the continuance of our existence" (p. 15).

do not teach us something new so much as they remind us of something we need to remember.

> Knowing is moving in tune with being. The implication is that what-is is neither formless or still. This is also what physics and biology have to tell us. It is not surprising, then, that these two domains of knowing were one with poetry to the presocratics, as they are in oral cultures around the world. They are one to us as well when we give up hope of owning, controlling, manipulating the world, and of living, like spoiled heirs, separately from the world on what the world provides. (Bringhurst, 1995, p. 53).

Pedagogy thinks by the way it moves. When teaching transmogrifies knowledge into preserved specimens for objective analysis and corrals being into a single human category, we experience learning and the world as monotonous. When teaching remediates the kinship between knowing and life as it is lived and attunes to the polyphony of being, we experience learning and the world as resonant. But this is real work, clearing away the accumulation of so much habit and desire but also contending with the troubling sense that we may not like what "resonant knowing" brings. "What kind of mushrooms are these?" Teacher holds his arms out as if to protect his students from slipping over an edge: "I am not sure, but they might be poisonous. Let's head back." Conversely, an ecopoetic pedagogy remains on the edge with strangeness, underground, in the liminal realm just beyond what is allowed to be expressed about more-than-human kinship (even when the wound of human supremacy may break our hearts [Martusewicz, 2014])—committed to acknowledging, mourning, and celebrating *what-is*. "Knowing is what, with love and humility, you *do*" (Dragland, 1995, p. 13).

Education as *applied* ecopoetics.

ॐ

Poet Dennis Lee continues: "A poem tries to enact that wordless tumble and surge in its own medium—in line breaks and pauses, syntax and sound, the ripple and clarion strut of sense on the page. It tries to recreate the cadence of how things are, through the nitty-gritty of craft" (2002, p. 19). In other words, a "good poem" thinks well because its carefully crafted prosody, resonant form and hand-picked metaphors are the imaginative yield of some disciplined practice of listening with the world before trying to say something definitive about it. There is a commitment to a kind of rigorous empiricism at play here, to a "lyric realism" (Zwicky, 2008) aimed at re-making resonant experiences, and thus reanimating the world for the reader, the interlocutor, or, as the case may be, the student. This practice is informed and honed by developing a disposition sensitive to the resonant structures of the world: the fit of human thought to the ecology of what-is, or put in more reciprocal terms, the attentive correlation of response and co-response.

> The 'experience' of truth is always the experience of resonance, that is, of attunement of various distinct components of a whole.
>
> This is not to say that everything that is true is also resonant. The sorts of truths pursued in analysis, for example, generally lack resonance.
>
> To say that an utterance is not resonant is not to say that it is not true. Rather, it is to say it has no phenomenology. (Zwicky, 2003, p. L37)

Educational research and practice initiated via systematic acts of severance to isolate the objective "empirical instance" from our lived experience also tend to lack resonance. This is *not* to claim that the sorts of truths pursued in analysis are not useful or even "enlightening," but when applied to pedagogical practice as it is lived, strict analysis can land as flat, distant, disconnected. This is education without craft or relation, this is the rigid transmission of prescribed learning objectives into hollowed vessels. Moreover, if logico-mathematical forms of thinking are systematically and artificially privileged, then *analysis* too loses its venerable poise as an insightful kind of knowing interconnected with living well and truthfully, and can mutate, by way of the education system, into an ecologically malignant desire for control, dominion and certainty. When the poetic generativity of earth and education is rendered by such desires, our sense of possibility, responsibility and care withers in the harsh light of "objective" surface description. As Jardine has maintained, when the earth loses its generative character, the subject loses its humility and humans lose our humanity (1998, pp. 9–10).

A pedagogical practice informed by "lyric realism," on the other hand, seeks to attune learning to what-is as a generative and imaginative process of "home-making" (*here*, entangled as we are with our more-than-human kin who also call this interspecies planet home). The ecopoetic educator, like the "good" nature poet, thus implors the nitty-gritty of form, pedagogical prosody and the possibility of address to clear and co-create a free space where we, perchance, may be called to recognize our kinship with things. In order to write, or begin to think about writing a composition, however, an ecologically minded poet must approach her practice, as Fisher-Wirth and Street have claimed with "attentiveness, precision, and a tenderness towards existence" (2013, p. xxvii). This orientation and the cultivation of these kinds of disciplines (i.e. "prep time") are important ecologically, not only because they acknowledge the rhythmic or poetic logic of thinking, or what David Abram (1996) has called the somatic dimension of language, but also the affective and gestural significance of more-than-human meaning.

> For meaning, as we have said, remains rooted in the sensory life of the body—it cannot be completely cut off from the soil of direct, perceptual experience without withering and dying.
>
> Yet to affirm that linguistic meaning is primarily expressive, gestural, and poetic, and that conventional and denotative meanings are inherently secondary and derivative, is to renounce the claim that "language" is an exclusively human property. If language is always, in its depths, physically and sensorially resonant, then it can never be definitively separated from the evident expressiveness of birdsong, or the evocative howl of a wolf late at night. (p. 80)

And if we are able to attune to the evident expressiveness of birdsong and wolf howl, why not with the subtler vibrations of the interlocutors beneath us? What would happen, for example, if we *seriously* considered what mycorrhizal mycelia *mean*? What if our consciousness was saturated by the mutualistic, interspecies and remedial implications? What would it mean to calibrate our understanding of the world with its symbiotic teachings? What are some of the implications of recognizing its cooperative co-evolutionary entanglement on the way we understand economics, ecology, education? What might we learn if we listened to the thrum beneath us?

It seems to me that an "ecopoetic practice"—the development of ecologically-attuned dispositions, sensitivities and disciplines—is an apposite undertaking for educators in an age of relational fragmentation. We require resonant pedagogies characterized by their attentiveness, precision and tenderness towards existence. Finding and making the free spaces to initiate, craft and discuss the development of these kinds of practices is important work, regardless of the myriad difficulties and heart-wrenching implications involved in translating "ecopoetic insights" to colleagues, students, and bureaucratic interlopers. The experience is something akin, I think, to being *moved* by a good piece of art, or perhaps a sublime sunset, but not being able to articulate why or, in other words, conceptually translate what the body understands in an instance. This can lead to irresolute accounts that do not "hold up" in civilized dialogue or institutional discourse. After all, when one attempts to articulate an experience of meaning in, for example, the way light can pierce a moment, or even something more workaday like the educational virtue of ambiguity, one is almost immediately met with the disdain of the objectivist—what about rigour, validity, measurement? "Yes, you must be right, it was only a silly poem, the end of another day, a moment of weakness."

> The phenomenology of experience is particularly relevant in situations where there is evidence that certain experiences are shared but also ignored by ideological emphases in the culture. Attending to their phenomenology is one way to begin to take them seriously; and to begin to reflect on the politics of their marginalization. (Zwicky, 2003, p. L109)

The conventional school experience, of course, plays a key role in marginalizing our experiences of more-than-human kinship. The "factory" or "big box" manifestations, in particular, seem to inculcate a second-guessing of our bodily intuitions, our emotionality, our innate sense of animate and participatory reciprocity with things (Abram, 1996; Evernden, 1993). The school, in its form, prosody and content, is a symbolic manifestation of the cultural logic of dominion and control—the desks in rows, the samples of individual work on the walls, the lingering smell of cleaning solvent in the hallways—everything conveys to students a particular way of understanding and being in the world (Creeping Snowberry & Blenkinsop, 2010). The nitty-gritty of ecopoetic pedagogy thus entails thoughtful attending to the phenomenology of marginalized or ineffable experiences with more-than-human alterity—despite the fact that bureaucratic teaching and learning systems dominate. In terms of curriculum, the ecopoetic teacher aims to craft (or perhaps "co-craft," as we cannot force an experience of resonance) an educational experience that invites ontological awareness by means of an "ecopoetic encounter." "Why have those leaves turned red?" The question hangs. Well, let's go have a look at this tree. What might the tree be communicating with these red, lantern-like leaves? What do the falling leaves sound like? What does it mean? When I ring the bell, I invite everyone to listen.

> This implies that the tree and leaves could hold the answer to the question, rather than a book or authoritative human figure. There is a recognition of the importance

of context along with a sense of complexity present here, allowing for a multiplicity of answers and new questions which may be pursued in various directions. (Creeping Snowberry & Blenkinsop, 2010, p. 58)

ॐ

Jardine has spelled out our collusion and obedience to objectivist methodologies in education as a result of the historical rise of univocal discourses in modernity. He explains that the paradigm of clarity in Western knowledge cannot allow for ambiguity, metaphorical speech, poetry or analogy. In other words: "A must equal A," or discourse must revolve around a single name. "To speak truly is to adhere to the univocal frontiers of things themselves (or to adhere to the univocal frontiers of reason itself which reproduces its own frontiers by constructing objects of knowledge in light of those frontiers)" (1998, p. 14). The intention here is not to let poetic and phenomenological fluff off the hook or to over-romanticize its affect. The point is to reiterate the hermeneutic insight that univocal discourses have been endowed with cultural-historical privilege in light of their own frontiers, not with objectively privileged access to reality. As such, strict adherence to the paradigm of clarity in educational theory represents a methodological choice, a forced fit with what is presently thinkable, not a disciplined commitment to "speak truly." An ecopoetic orientation, in this sense, acts again as a reminder that there can also be a kind of wisdom in ambiguity, a truth speaking that resonates with what lived experience shows, a disciplined, rigorous and lyrically empirical validity (this is, in fact, what is required in order to sense resonant structures).

> Ambiguity is the world's condition. Poetry flirts with ambiguity. As a "picture of reality" it is truer than any other. Ambiguity is. This doesn't mean you're supposed to write poems no one understands. (Simic, 1990, p. 88)

But Charles Simic is a Pulitzer Prize winning poet, so of course, for him, poetry's flirtations with what-is seem truer than any other. Let's abandon grand or comparative truth claims for a moment and return instead to the real problem: the demand for univocal certainty in discourse. In this regard, Zwicky (2003) is much closer to the mark, describing our methodical elimination of ambiguity in terms of an addiction and pointing towards the "real discovery:"

> The real discovery is not the one that will let us stop doing philosophy when we want to. Philosophy is thinking in love with clarity; and such thinking, in itself, is not a source of problems. What will not let us rest is the thought that what is clear must also be single; we are addicted to the elimination of ambiguity. If a thing is *truly* the path down, we think, it cannot also truly be the path up; at least one of these, we say, must be merely an appearance.
>
> But this is not to think clearly. It is to fail to attend to what experience shows. It is to stop short of wisdom, which recognizes clarities that non-metaphorical language cannot render. Different wholes occupy the same space.
>
> The real discovery is the one that will let philosophy resume thinking metaphorically when it needs to. (Zwicky, 2003, p. L116)

What about rigour, validity, measurement? Yes these things are important and useful, as is a healthy dollop of reductionism, depending on the project and context. An ecopoetic approach does not suggest that quantitative educational research be composed as haiku. Methodological strategies perform important functions and can be insightful in their own ways. An ecopoetic education is not anti-philosophy, anti-science or even anti-reductionism. Critically speaking, it is a move to deliquesce the rigidity of culturally and historically privileged modes of understanding; to get out from inquiry as the desire for rule and control and recognize what calls for questions in a world of ecological emergency.

২

The hermeneutic experience for Jardine is an earthly encounter; an ecological address at the substratum of thinking that we experience as being *drawn out* of our subjectivity, our our-centeredness, into a teeming world of living relations.

> What addresses us does so from beyond our wanting and doing, beyond our constructs. We experience the limits of our experience by experiencing something that calls us to go beyond the limits of experience. Less philosophically put, we live in a world and that world houses us and our thinking and experiencing. We do not house it in our constructs. This, of course, is an *ecological* and a *pedagogical* point as much as it is a commentary on research methodologies in education. (2006, p. 271)

The ecopoetic mind knows thinking is always already *housed*.[2] It derives wisdom from the sense that the world and thinking itself have limits that cannot be distorted indefinitely despite our wanting and doing. To try and house the world

---
2   In the etymological sense of *eco-*, as in the Greek root *oikos*, as in *house* or *household*.

in ecologically destructive constructs is to force fit thinking and risk epistemic ossification and invariably, extinction. Conversely, lyric thinking attempts to fit with the world and attune to its patterned resonance; to remain fluid, attentive, open to participatory reciprocity and, of course, to live accordingly. To not only accumulate knowledge, but cultivate wisdom.

Zwicky (2003) describes wisdom as "a form of domestic understanding" (p. L96) and has maintained, "To know the meaning of what-is is wisdom" (p. L86). If being is the manifest interrelatedness of things, then human thought in attunement with what-is is a form of housed or ecological reason. One is tempted to use the term "ecological understanding" as is common in sustainability education initiatives, but here we must be careful not to conflate ecological knowledge with wisdom. One must know something about the world and its relations in order to be wise about the home, but ecological wisdom is attained through *allowing* the world to think through oneself over and above wanting and doing. This is real and humbling work which entails not superimposing anthropic constructs onto the world to force it to yield to consumptive desires. This move does not, however, subsume individuality (per se), particularity or difference. As environmental theorist Mick Smith (2001a) has written, "One does not need to espouse an isolated conception of an autonomous and bounded subject in order to argue that we are, to a degree, self-constructed, internally motivated and so on. The world does not just speak through us" (p. 224). Rather wisdom recognizes that we belong to a community of beings with voice and perspective and we come to understand the world—even to understand *human*—by attuning to the other-than-human.

Ambiguity is the world's condition. Perhaps then, a sense of the significance of ambiguity may be in order when we attempt to correlate our ideas with the voice of the world. Put another way, there can be wisdom in ambiguity, a kind of honesty in responding to the ever-shifting cadence of what-is. And the practice of wisdom? Of course there are many schools and traditions one might draw upon here, but a sense of attending thoughtfully and carefully to things seems to lie near the heart of most. Despite his failed attempts at being a school teacher, Wittgenstein (2009, p. 36) offers a compendious little axiom for an ecopoetic pedagogy:

To repeat: don't think, but look!

So much of our experience is fragmented, severed and hyperseparated by the cultural-historical norms of discourse we acquire through schooling. Ecopoetic thinking attempts to keep connections between realms of discourse and between human and more-than-human open, dynamic and, for lack of a better term, critically relevant to the issues of the day. It calls attention to the co-existence of diverse epistemological orientations and implies that our ability to travel between them echoes, in a sense, the interrelated structure of the world itself. The reverse is also true, and an important philosophic aspect of ecological education; which is to say, drawing attention to the interrelatedness of ecological relations ought to ideally lead to a more reflexive understanding of the analogical relations and kinship between realms of discourse (Jardine, 1998).

Despite an obvious concern with aesthetic experience[3] and poetics, it would be a mistake to read ecohermeneutics as an "aesthetic theory." Ecopoïesis is not aesthetic experience *about* the world per se, but poetic encounter *with* the world, from *within* the flux, and intended to draw one into awareness of the ethics of an interspecies entangled world. In this sense, adding the prefix *eco-* to *poïesis* (or *hermeneutics* for that matter) is way of recognizing that thinking is always *housed* and perception *shared*. An ecopoetic education is a means of imploying aesthetic experience to clear the space for this insight. To prepare, by training the attention, for the possibility of such an act.

The rest follows of itself.

ॐ

What does an ecopoetic understanding of education really mean for teaching on the ground? How does the pedagogy *move*—on the page, in the classroom,

---

3   For an insightful discussion on what is meant by "aesthetic experience" and why Gadamer discusses aesthetic experience as an introduction to the nature of philosophical hermeneutics see Jardine (2006). Aesthetic experience here is not simply "art appreciation" or a study of "good poetry," but an attempt to describe those rich and memorable experiences that catch our attention and ask things of us, those questions that the world *presses upon us*. "This is what Gadamer means by suggesting that, at the core of hermeneutics, at the core of 'what happens to us over and above our wanting and doing,' is something akin to an 'aesthetic experience.' Aesthetic experience, Gadamer suggests, is the experience of being drawn out of our subjectivity and into the teeming world of relations that lives 'beyond our wanting and doing.' The task posed to understanding at such a juncture cannot be simply one of corralling that teeming world back into the confines of our constructs" (p. 271).

beyond the schoolyard fence? What does a lyric-minded educator *do*? Zwicky has claimed, "Other than pointing and hoping, there are no rules, no algorithms, by which human perception of a gestalt may be facilitated" (2003, p. L117). Initially, this may seem unacceptably passive; is there nothing more we can do as educators other than point and hope? How many times have I taken groups of students into the forest, pointing at the rings of severed trees and lifting logs to expose the gossamer tufts of mycelia, hoping that they would come to understand that *this* tree and *this* soil really exist, or rather we all *co-exist*. That these things are connected and symbiotic with each other and there are lessons to be learned here—hoping the rest would follow of itself.

More often than not, students are already conditioned to think about the world as essentially meaningless inert matter and think of themselves as autonomous and definitively bounded beings. Worse yet, some barely notice the change of environment, being too engrossed in hand-held electronic devices to pay attention to silly things like trees and "gross white stuff" under logs. Even if they are begrudgingly compelled to ask: "what kind of tree is this?" I fear that what they really mean is: "what is the taxonomic categorization of this organism?" Or perhaps, "what is this natural resource used for?" Or even, "how much is this tree worth? How many board feet of useful lumber are in this tree? If we cut this tree down, how much money do you think we could we get for it?" (This suspicion is of course reinforced by the signage that sometimes accompanies trees that "stand out" and tends to provide this kind of information—"Look, this ring indicates when 'Columbus discovered America'"—*sigh*).

In a sense, there is *always* an element of pointing and hoping when attempting to tune the mind to rhythmic logics, ontological appreciation cannot be forced or inculcated. This is, in essence, the same conundrum explored by eco-educational philosopher Sean Blenkinsop (2005) in his discussion of philosopher Martin Buber and the impossibility of forcing an I/Thou relationship in education. "Buber agreed that the moment of change, or the moment of insight, can't be forced into existence and must come from and to the student, as if by grace, but that does not mean that we do nothing to prepare, to set the stage consciously for when the moment arrives" (p. 292). So while there may always be an element of pointing and hoping, we should do all that we can to prepare for the possibility. Attentiveness is an active, conscious and intentional discipline. As Zwicky (2003) has maintained, "There is a psychological element here, as well as a talent for seeing-as. One has to be able to see what *is* there, rather than what one hopes or expects. This requires a certain sort of strength" (p. L95). And more specifically, "That practice is better understood as an exercise of attention disciplined by

Chapter Three   39

discernment of the live, metaphorical relation between things and the resonant structure of the world" (p. L117). How, then, might we think about preparing for, and maybe even coaxing, the possibility of a mycelial moment? What kind of philosophic and practice-based moves do we have to make before resonant logic becomes thinkable? More pressing, perhaps, what does it mean in a time of ecological emergency if educators bend their own ears to the world and hear nothing but the monotone hubbub and immutable drone of the anthropos?

I want to say something like: one cannot teach what one *is* not. Or put differently, the most important and consistent thing we teach is *who we are*. Although the ontological nature of teaching is emphasized in each, both statements seem too passively uniform, too subjective, too gnawingly anthropocentric. I want to say critical self-reflexivity is an ecological imperative in the practice of teaching today, but this also seems too shallow and self-evident. There are two paths, which are really two aspects or threads of a single *way of thinking*—the deliquescent and the remedial, or the "ecocritical" and the "ecopoetic." Ecohermeneutics demands that one walk this path beyond our present horizon of understanding, and as must be the case, teacher before student. This line of questioning will decidedly lead one beyond a stereotypical "environmental education": picking up litter, recycling neighborhood aluminum cans, writing letters to local politicians to save a city park. Primarily it involves learning to hear the questions properly, to listen to what the world means above and beyond our wanting and doing. Our responses take us beyond educational theory into the realms of ethics, politics, livelihood, of existential possibility, but first we must learn to listen.

Hear.

ॐ

Writing in another discipline, literary critic Northrop Frye had this to say on the often-paradoxical ideals we are faced with as educators: "The English teacher's ideal is the exact opposite of 'effective communication,' or learning to become audible in the market place. What he has to teach is the verbal expression of truth, beauty and wisdom: in short, the disinterested use of words" (1988, p. 26). Borrowing from Frye, we might say: the ecopoetic teacher's ideal is the exact opposite of "sustainable development," or learning how to compete for voice in the market place of green solutions. What she has to teach is discernment of the live, metaphorical relation between things and the resonant structure of the world: in short, the identity of poetry and thinking. This is both a deliquescent and a remedial task. According to Bringhurst (2006), the vocation of the teacher is just this, inoculating the hum of being "well-adjusted" with strange fruiting bodies and the spawn of wildness.

> The *school* may indeed exist for the purpose of adjusting the student to society. But the *teacher* exists for the purpose of frustrating that adjustment. Why? Because vocation is better than adjustment, and the two are not the same. Vocation is articulate; adjustment hums along. But why, in a healthy society, should vocation be a form of maladjustment? Because society is never healthy in that sense. Health in society *means* that maladjustment can be fruitful. (p. 54)

The Ecological-Ontology of Education 101 is not a required course you somehow missed in teachers college between *classroom management* and *methods of assessment*. In fact, the process of becoming educated in modern Western culture could, in part, be described as the time-honoured process of severing our mindbodies from ecological relations by silencing the *voice* of the more-than-human. Evernden (1993) referred to this modern educational "rite of passage" as a process of attaining "sufficient detachment," a process that culminates in the ultimate act of the vivisectionist—"severing the vocal cords of the world" (p. 16). Jardine (1998) echoes these sentiments with similar imagery: "All the ambiguous ways in which things were experienced to be out there cannot withstand…methodical doubt. The living Earth and our lives together withdraw into silence" (pp. 20–21).

This severance is achieved, in part, by corralling the experience of meaning into a phenomenon exclusively shared between human interlocutors. The metaphysical foundations of the Western tradition are, in a sense, based in dismembering meaning from the hermeneutic significance of more-than-human form. We are schooled in methodical doubt (and forced to sit still, in rows, inside a pedagogical apparatus designed to carry the effects of power to those who attend in order to alter behaviour [Foucault, 1979]) until most of us resoundingly mistrust, suppress and self-censor the "body's silent conversation with things" (Abram, 1996, p. 49).

For Abram,[4] the first step in remediating this severance is acknowledging the body as "the very means of entering into relation with all things" (p. 46).

---

4   Merleau-Ponty himself never attempted a phenomenology of reading and writing, nor did he explicitly address "environmental theory" per se; however, Abram's interpretation (1996) of his work strikes me as an exceptional example of ecohermeneutic interpretation or what

> To acknowledge that "I am this body" is not to reduce the mystery of my yearnings and fluid thoughts to a set of mechanisms, or my "self" to a determinate robot. Rather it is to affirm the uncanniness of the physical form. It is not to lock up awareness within the density of a closed and bounded object, for as we shall see, the boundaries of a living body are open and indeterminate; more like membranes than barriers, they define a surface of metamorphosis and exchange. The breathing, sensing body draws its sustenance and its very substance from the soils, plants, and elements that surround it; it continually contributes itself, in turn, to the air, to the composting earth, to the nourishment of insects and oak trees and squirrels, ceaselessly spreading out of itself as well as breathing the world into itself, so that it is very difficult to discern, at any moment, precisely where this living body begins and where it ends. (pp. 46-47)
>
> Communicative meaning is always, in its depths, affective; it remains rooted in the sensual dimension of experience, born of the body's native capacity to resonate with other bodies and with the landscape as a whole. Linguistic meaning is not some ideal and bodiless essence that we arbitrarily assign to a physical sound or word and then toss out into the "external" world. Rather, meaning sprouts in the very depths of the sensory world, in the heat of meeting, encounter, participation. (p. 75)

Acknowledging the sensuous world as a source of human cognition and the importance of somatic understanding is an important insight, but obviously *something has happened*. Something has precipitated an estrangement with the world and left the modern Western mind alienated from the "natural world" despite our tacit biophysical interface. It is true, in a sense, the body is the means of entering into relationship with all things, an idea shared, in essence, by Bringhurst: "The mind is part of the body, the body is part of the world, and the world is part of the mind" (2006, p. 52). And while I agree with the notion, I am troubled, pedagogically speaking, by the body's so-called "native capacity to resonate with other bodies and with the landscape as a whole" (Abram, 1996, p. 75). Or perhaps the wording of this statement has become worrying in light of the dominance of Piagetian models of development in education and the search for a "biologized" nature of mind that downplays or eliminates the sociocultural significance of development (Egan, 2002; also see Judson, 2010). The fear is that if meaning is understood as rooted in the sensual dimension as a "native capacity," a kind of genetic hardwiring that develops in the process of normal organismic growth; then perhaps, as the logic goes, we simply need to just get "culture" out of the way? Perhaps we just need to "get kids outside" and let

---

might be deemed *ecoexegesis*. Although not framed in these terms, his poetic interweaving of ecological ethics, interconnectivity, the ecology of language and the importance of orality comprise a rigorously lyrical ecohermeneutic rendering.

our "native capacities" resonate? While this may sound absurd, this is precisely the kind of romanticized understanding of the educative potential of "nature" that drives many ecological education initiatives today (Fettes, 2013; Derby, Blenkinsop, Telford, Piersol & Caulkins, 2013).

I share in the fundamental point Abram is making, the body is biophysically and perceptually immersed in the world, and on some level, *all* communicative meaning is sensuous. The critical task of ecohermeneutics is coupling sensuous encounters with, as Abram has gone to great lengths to illustrate, awareness of the importance of thoughtful sociocultural and linguistic mediation (or, clearing the attentive space for *ecopoïesis* by means of such mediation). An ecopoetic education does not only seek somatic immersion in a narrow sense (it does not just get kids outside), and it does not suggest that linguistic mediation can be simply "set aside" (there should be, of course, space and time for contemplative practices, which may yield ineffable experiences, but the bulk of our educational experiences will entail linguified reflection, debriefing, and articulation) (Fettes, 2013). Although intimately related to somatic understanding, there is an emphasis in ecohermeneutics on developing the capacity to think metaphorically as both a means to critically distanciate from ontological presuppositions and ideological emphases in the dominant culture and to come into intimate "ecopoetic" attunement with ecological form.

> Metaphor is one way of showing how patterns of meaning in the world intersect and echo one another. The ability to think analogically is a reflection of sensitivity to ontological form. (Zwicky, 2003, p. L6)

We turn our attention now to metaphor.

chapter four

metaphor & thinking with *this* bird

Metaphor is a way of understanding the world; it comes naturally to nearly all language-speakers. Any account that makes it out to be odd or queer in relation to "the norm" is itself odd or queer. We think we need such an account only because we have misconstrued the nature of 'the norm.' A good account will be as much a critique of standard Western assumptions about meaning's relation to language as it will be a positive discussion of metaphor. (Zwicky, 2003, p. L115)

Imagination is neither the language of nature nor the language of man, but both at once, the medium of communication between the two—as if the birds, unable to understand the speech of man, and man, unable to understand the songs of birds, yet longing to communicate, were to agree on a tongue made up of sounds they both could comprehend—the voice of running water perhaps or the wind in the trees. Imagination is the *elemental speech* in all senses, the first and the last, of primitive man and of the poets. (Goddard, 1951, p. 10)

The education system is one of the pivotal institutions responsible for the reproduction of cultural norms and has thus, by and large, maintained the culture of denial with respect to the consequences of rendering earth a cornucopian storehouse (Bowers, 1997; see also Orr, 1991; Prakash & Esteva, 2008; Gruenewald & Smith, 2008; Jardine, 2012). Ironically, it is also the social institution most often charged with "solving" the environmental problem; an impending concern that seems to loom ominously on the horizon, but never imminently enough to effectuate any real transformation of the dominant neoliberal ethos (Gruenewald & Manteaw, 2007; Hursh & Henderson, 2011;

McKenzie, 2012). The cultural-historical dimension of the environmental crisis—the way received patterns of belief have resulted in exploitative use-relations with things—is rarely discussed in schools or the public sphere (Martusewicz et al., 2011). Instead, the environmental problem tends to be framed as an inconvenient hitch, that will, given time and interminable human innovation, be solved with an exciting new array of green-bio-nano-technologies, upgraded resource management techniques, and, of course, a move towards "education for sustainable development."[1] But while environmental issues such as climate change and the bioaccumulation of toxins have been tacked on to the science curriculum, the mythopoetics of progress, technological optimism and human exceptionalism remain deep-seated. The modern school is retrofitted with energy-saving lightbulbs, some raised garden beds and a professional development day devoted to the environmental virtues of electronic portfolios, but the foundational metaphors remain concealed and intact.

Conversely, Blenkinsop (2012) digs right into the foundations of the matter, asserting that the education system sits at the "vanguard" of our environmentally destructive and socially unjust worldview, and if we are to effect cultural change, we must address the non-environmental, if not anti-environmental, roots of the crisis inherent within modernity. As previous chapters have suggested, working on the level of metaphor is essential if we are to dig to the cultural substratum. Blenkinsop and Fettes (2009) suggest that we need to explore educational projects aimed explicitly at cultural change by drawing upon the work of ecophilosophers (Evernden, 1993; Abram, 1996; Jardine, 1998), ecofeminists (Plumwood, 1993; Fawcett, 2000) and ecojustice educators (Bowers, 2008a; Martusewicz et al., 2011) who all maintain that, on some level, the problem lies in the very metaphors upon which Western culture is mythopoetically sustained. Furthermore, in colonial situations, these transformative place-based projects must be thoughtfully integrated with ecologically minded critical theory (Gruenewald, 2003; Kahn, 2010; Lewis & Kahn, 2010) and, if possible, appropriate and enacted with "ethical relationality" (a topic further explored in chapter eight), entwined with Indigenous pedagogies of decolonization (Cajete, 1994; Chambers, 1999; Donald, 2009; Four Arrows, 2013; Battiste, 2013).

Environmental education initiatives—ostensibly the corrective to our culture of denial—are all too often "experientially focused" (this is to say focused on

---

1   See Huckle and Wals (2015) for an analysis of the literature supporting the UN Decade for Education for Sustainable Development and a sample of its key products which suggest that it failed to acknowledge neoliberalism as a hegemonic force and has resulted in business as usual in the end.

"experiential activities" such as canoeing or geocaching, not what comprises a meaningful pedagogic "experience" with the more-than-human world) and have tended to lack a robust developmental framework, a philosophy of language, contemplative depth, imaginative and arts-based emphases and ecocritical-cultural analysis. When the project of cultural transformation, including a focus on the significance of the linguistic and metaphoric dimension of the ecological crisis, is absent, one is led to wonder whether these initiatives subtly, yet fundamentally, work to reinforce dominant presuppositions (or perhaps provide false hope, which is itself a powerful kind of denial) despite their well-meaning, eco-friendly mandates?

ॐ

What does it mean, then, to work with metaphor at the level of cultural transformation? One of the objectives of this work is becoming critically aware of the ontological presuppositions manifest as the very material and structural constituents of the "typical" experience in our schools. Blenkinsop offers some observations as to the subtle ways in which the metaphoric dimension operates in educational programs:

> As we all do, our students live immersed in a plethora of social and cultural messages. The structure and function of schools tells us what is important and what is not, what to be aware of and what to ignore, how systems work, and how the culture works… the point is that these messages reflect the culture. Within schools, environmental education may be undone by the conflicting messages created by these cultural artefacts. For example, a teacher may spend the day discussing interdependence, then a bell sounds summoning students to a different classroom and a different discipline, or homework is returned with each student receiving an individual, independent mark. Such mixed metaphors are all too common, and a major challenge has been to try to find metaphors appropriate to an ecologically based education. What are we saying to the community when we use metaphors? What are their effects—positive or negative—and how does one underpin or undermine the effect of metaphors? (2012, p. 11)

Many environmental education programs, in addition to either disregarding or remaining unaware of the importance of work at the level of metaphor, do not adequately acknowledge the role imagination plays in engendering "ecological understanding" (Judson, 2010). If the aim is to engender a sense of humankind's "implicatedness in life" (Orr, 2005, p. 105), not simply provide, for example, more information about the interaction of biotic and abiotic factors in an ecosystem, or on the other hand, a positive "nature experience" in the great outdoors, then surely we must pay more attention to the distinctive features of our somatic, emotional and imaginative experience, particularly in such an aggressively ideological society.

Judson suggests we are in need of an "*ecological* conception of imagination" informed by an understanding of human embeddedness in the world and characterized by a flexibility of mind oriented to interdependence, pattern and complexity (2010, p. 5). Educating for an ecological imagination involves eliciting connection to the natural environment via narrative, place-based activities and learning opportunities that engage bodies, emotions and imaginative possibilities. But, as both Judson and Blenkinsop have reiterated, imagination is shaped by the cultural-historical contexts in which we are immersed, so, while maybe it goes without saying, it is important to reiterate that educating for an ecological imagination must always be, in a sense, educating for a "critical" socio-ecological imagination (Gruenewald, 2003; Kahn, 2010). A critical place-based pedagogy aimed at engaging and cultivating ecological imagination is, broadly speaking, also the objective of an ecohermeneutic approach, but the challenge of metaphor remains. How does one undermine, or rather deliquesce, the effects of those hypostatized metaphors that currently dominate (i.e., world as "natural resource")? Moreover, how does one provoke metaphors that, as Zwicky has described, enact a gesture of healing; that "pull a stitch through the rift that our capacity for language opens between us and the world" (2003, p. L59)?

This brings us to the important and perennial issue of what comprises a "critical" act when working on the level of metaphor in education. The tendency for those who approach education with a desire to *conscientize* has been to inform the other straightforwardly of their ideologically-laden assumptions. "Hey, the world is not just 'natural resources,' that is a capitalist logic used to rationalize an exploitative hegemony." Which is true, or rather it is one way of looking at it. But these educational approaches can sometimes prove a little frustrating because, as D. Smith (1999) has claimed, the interest of the critical tradition has not just been persuasion but a predetermination to shape the social order in fixed directions that seem perhaps too ideal or distortion-free for those with more of a "hermeneutic" sensibility.

On the other hand, the critical theorist's frustration "resides precisely in the very ambiguity and complexity of language which hermeneutics tries to uphold" (p. 37). This is by no means a condemnation of critical theory—the addition of the modifier *critical* to ecohermeneutics in this project is intentional, spirited and in solidarity with the important work conducted in that tradition (a topic explored further in chapter seven)—but rather a reiteration of the importance of clearing dialogical, relational and openended space for critical inquiry, especially in the realm of education. As Gadamer reminds us, "The task of life in general is to find free spaces and learn to move therein" (as cited in Jardine, 2012, pp. 1–2). Conscientization is still the objective, but critical consciousness is deepened when woven from collective and multivocal understandings with ethical relationality between human and more-than-human cultures (Donald, 2009). An ecohermeneutic attention attends to the distinctive features of our emotional and imaginative lives as they already are together. This necessarily involves bringing out the ambiguous, complex and humus-laden interweavings between self and other, and self and more-than-human other. Critical consciousness from an ecohermeneutic perspective entails a constant and reflexive discipline of rethinking what is at work in particular ways of speaking and acting in order to facilitate ever-deepening appreciation of the wholeness and integrity of the world which must be present for thought and action to be possible at all (D. Smith, 1999, p. 37). The process of naming the ways in which our language may carry an environmentally destructive residue is an important undertaking, but metaphors can never really be cleansed once and for all, others will always understand differently. The objective of critique in ecohermeneutic work is to imploy metaphor to clear space for deep relational possibilities and let the ethic emerge from within and follow of itself. This does not, as I see it, conflict with prefigurative political gestures, but rather generates the relational basis for dialogue concerning an evolving (interspecies) praxis.

ৡ

Let's return to an ecopoetic understanding of education, that is, an educational practice aimed at the cultivation of ecocritical thought by/and eliciting attention to the resonant structures of interrelatedness. As we have seen, an ecopoetic approach shares in the idea that working with metaphor is one of the primary means of attending to both our historically effected consciousness (Gadamer, 2013) and the lived phenomenology of experience. But digging to the mythopoetic roots of a culture and oneself is difficult work; not only does it entail cultivating a discipline for seeing-as but, as Blenkinsop has illustrated, a subtle and diligent awareness of the pedagogic significance of artefact, environment and gesture. What's more, because objectivist approaches have relegated "imaginative" experience to the realm of idle fantasy, artistic self-expression or trivial novelty, we are often made to feel strange in considering interpretive practices as legitimate pedagogical concerns (Egan, 1997; Jardine, 1998).

In response to such archaic positions, as well as any lingering diffidence in our schooled habits of mind, recall the sentiments of eminent hermeneutical thinker Wilhelm Dilthey, when he suggested that "feeling strange or alien" is the first prerequisite to a life of interpretation (as cited in D.G. Smith, 1999, p. xiv). Educational philosopher Maxine Greene has echoed these sentiments suggesting that no teacher can avoid critically examining her presuppositions as a stranger. The "stranger's vantage point" is something like "returning home from a long stay in some other place;" the homecoming teacher may begin to notice details and patterns in her environment she never saw before (1973, pp. 267-268). Welcome home.

> Be aware: Things might get strange.

ৡ

The cultivation of ecocritical skills and modes of analysis is fundamental to an ecohermeneutic imagination, but as Zwicky has maintained, "Critique, too, is empty unless the space it clears becomes home to insight" (2003, p. L21). Working at the level of metaphor provides educators a powerful means to clear space, or in keeping with thinking with fungi, to deliquesce hypostatized epistemicides and mycoremediate the intellectual landscape. This means working with metaphor's ability to acknowledge, mourn and celebrate the world within the places where education happens.

> The artefacts, symbols, and touchstones of modernity that are the source of our ecological crisis are at play in the fabric of our educational institutions and practices; they are the water in which we swim, they form the fishbowl of our reality. They can be discovered, not just through detached theoretical analysis—whether it be sociological, philosophical, or critical cultural in nature—but through actual engaged awareness within the places where education happens. Further, fostering careful awareness of these messages which bombard our senses and which shape the ways in which we come to understand and act in the world is a vital consideration... (Creeping Snowberry & Blenkinsop, 2010, pp. 53-54)

Reflecting on Hannah Arendt's claim that education is the point at which we decide whether we "love the world" enough to assume responsibility for it,

Chapter Four

Maxine Greene has suggested that even pondering what it signifies to "love the world" is to move beyond theoretical analysis into domains where poets ordinarily venture. "And to save the world from ruin, to cherish it, must involve those who attend in metaphorical thinking: the linking of what is apparently unlike, bringing together disparate ideas, enriching and expanding both" (1988, pp. 51-52). For Greene, the function of metaphor in education, and by extension imagination, is something like a public dialogue that incorporates multiperspectivalism and focuses on democracy, political agency and freedom. Again, while this is a crucially important aspect of metaphoric thinking to develop, when Creeping Snowberry and Blenkinsop (2010) refer to the "ecosemiotics of education" and the fostering of an "engaged awareness within the places where education happens" they are referring more to the ontological domain of metaphor where *good* poets venture. Eliciting ontological attention is, as I have claimed, the keystone task of ecohermeneutics. To recognize that this dungy dirt underneath this log here, this decaying woodland chanterelle, this bird (the squawking corvid, the old crow there to the right

this bird, *here*

exists as much as you do is a form of love.

> When we love a thing, we can experience our responsibility toward it as limitless (the size of the world). Responsibility is the trace, in us, of the pressure of the world that is focused in a *this*. That is *how much* it is possible to attend; that is how large complete attention would be. (Zwicky, 2003, p. L57)

ৡ

Before we delve any deeper into metaphor's capacity to refocus ontological attention, let's first establish its crucial role in intellectual development. The relationship between metaphor and thought is one of those enigmatic subjects that has concerned scholars for millennia (see Barfield, 2011; Cazeaux, 2007; Sacks, 1978). For our purposes, and with respect to metaphor's pedagogical significance, I shall draw primarily on the research of Simon Fraser University's Imaginative Education Research Group (Egan, 1997; Blenkinsop, 2009; Judson, 2010; Nielsen, Fitzgerald & Fettes, 2010) and share in educational philosophers Kieran Egan's observation that both the pervasiveness of metaphor in language use and young children's fluency and recognition of metaphor is something that educators should find centrally important (1997, p. 54). This rather obvious sentiment is, regrettably, important to reiterate being that there is relatively little attention paid to the importance of metaphor in educational research compared to more logico-mathematical forms of thinking.

Imaginative Education employs a cognitive tools approach to intellectual development (although it must be noted that "cognitive" development is always tied to some degree to an embodied or somatic core of understanding) and situates metaphor as one of the cognitive tools that we acquire through oral language use to make sense of the world. Although Egan (1997) does not describe his project as "hermeneutic," there is a hermeneutic quality to the polysemous "kinds of understandings" he describes as we internalize culturally mediated tools. By "cognitive tools," Egan is referring to something like the "mediational means" of Russian psychologist Lev Vygotsky (1986), who proposed that intellectual development cannot be adequately understood in terms of straightforward knowledge accumulation or innate psychological stages, but requires an understanding of the role played by the intellectual tools available in any society or historical situation to make sense of things. Thus, the set of sign systems that one internalizes from interacting within particular cultural groups or communities of discourse will significantly inform one's kind of understanding (Egan, 1997, pp. 29-30). From a cognitive tools perspective, education is best conceived of as the acquisition of these intellectual toolkits and the development of each kind of understanding to its fullest potential as we engage first with oral language ("mythic understanding"), then literacy ("romantic understanding"), theoretic abstractions ("philosophic understanding") and finally the linguistic reflexiveness that yields radical epistemic doubt and the coalescence of all previous kinds of understandings ("ironic understanding").[2]

Beyond its universal prevalence in language, metaphor is acknowledged as a particularly rich intellectual tool due to its generative ability to establish new relationships between heterogeneous ideas in a way that adds something to, or throws new light on, the topic. As Egan has claimed, "Expansion of understanding seems often to ride on the kind of generative grasp one finds exemplified in metaphor—and that, again, follows a logic quite different from the content associations so prominent in educational textbooks" (1997, p. 55). In focusing on the generative aspect of metaphor, an aspect also noted by Greene (1988), Egan calls into question the false dichotomy between logic and metaphor, or more broadly speaking, reason and imagination, and resituates metaphoric

---

2 Imaginative Education will be addressed in more detail in chapter six.

ability as a vitally productive feature of constructive thought. We are left with the sense that, to some extent, fluent and flexible metaphor control is required for nearly all forms of thinking; or put in as simple terms as possible, as English literary critic I.A. Richards has written, "Thought is metaphoric, and proceeds by comparison [seeing one thing in terms of another], and the metaphors of language derive therefrom" (as cited in Egan, 1997, p. 58). Ultimately, for Egan, metaphors are *"bon à penser"*—a term coined by anthropologist Claude Levi-Strauss—implying that they are "good for thinking with" and although the ambiguous and irrational logic of metaphor is oftentimes anathema to modern Western minds, we would do well in education to develop an appreciation for its complexity and perspicuity. Egan has maintained that metaphor is "one of the foundations of all our mental activity, upon which our systematic logics of rational inquiry also rest, or—a better metaphor—the soil out of which they grow" (1987, p. 456). What might it mean then to bring these pedagogical insights on the role of metaphor to bear on ecological education?

ৡ

In her ecological approach to Imaginative Education, Judson (2010) builds on the work of Egan (1997), and offers a glimpse of how we might think in practical terms about the curricular role of metaphor in a Grade 8 class studying hummingbirds. Central to this approach is embedding the student's learning within an emotionally and imaginatively engaging narrative about the elegance and the truly remarkable powers of flight of this tiny creature—hummingbird as fearless flier. Teaching as storytelling is a central feature of Imaginative Education due to the way narrative shapes knowledge by bringing out its emotional force (Egan, 1997). This is particularly important for Judson as she recognizes that ecological understanding has an emotional core and learning about ecological processes and principles is only made meaningful by means of emotional attachment to real things in the "natural world" (2010, p. 1). Metaphor here is a powerful learning tool that comprises both a constitutive element of narratives and an indispensable cognitive tool to evoke emotional connection to the topic.

In Imaginative Ecological Education the pedagogical narrative is supplemented by learning about hummingbirds in ways that meaningfully engage students' bodies (which includes getting outside the classroom, but does not necessarily require this) and by developing what Judson has called "place-making cognitive tools" (2010, pp. 65-97; also see Fettes & Judson, 2011).

> They [students] are encouraged to employ their senses in observing the rhythms of the hummingbird, the great speed of its wings, the sound a bird's wing movement creates, the directionality of its flight. They are given opportunities to become hummingbirds. They express in various ways, from this new perspective what the world looks and feels like.... They explore the musicality of birds, playing with ways to recreate the music created by the rapidity of hummingbird wings in motion...researching more about this species. What makes this species unique? The hummingbird is a fearless flier—what makes a robin, bluejay, or crow unique? (Judson, 2010, pp. 2-3)

In this way, Judson claims the natural interdisciplinarity of the curriculum emerges and students are inspired to branch off and study other birds and related topics discovered whilst attending to hummingbirds. For example, the study of migration routes might draw connections to geography; the study of bird flight may draw connections to gravity or evolution, and observations about the unique beak of the hummingbird might draw connections to pollination, food security or sustainability issues. Students are also encouraged to explore the metaphoric dimension of birds via cultural idioms and proverbs; for instance, what does it mean when something is "for the birds" or if someone is said to have a "bird brain" or that "birds of a feather stick together" (p. 3)?

Cognitive tools, in Egan's formulation, bring together three components that tend to be addressed separately in educational theory: the epistemological, the psychological, and the emotional. There is little doubt that metaphor as a cognitive tool provides an effective means for rich intellectual development as it is tied up with knowledge comprehension and generation, but also in engaging our much-neglected emotional and imaginative lives (Judson, 2010, p. 37). The hummingbird as fearless flier lesson provides a practical and thoughtful example of metaphor's capacity in this regard—linking what is apparently unlike, bringing together disparate ideas, even providing opportunities to "become" hummingbirds and play with interspecies mimesis—but metaphor's capacity to elicit *ontological* attention is either downplayed or impoverished in its formulation as just another cognitive tool in the toolkit.

Focusing on the importance of somatic understanding and the natural interdisciplinarity of the curriculum is crucial "epistemologically," but critical ecohermeneutics also endeavours to elicit ontological sensitivity. These things are obviously not independent, but ecohermeneutics holds that, on some level, interdisciplinarity and our ability to reflexively move between different kinds of understanding are epistemic manifestations or echoes of some deeper ecology of meaning immanent in the world itself. Or as Zwicky (2003) has claimed in more lucid terms, "the ability to think analogically is a reflection of sensitivity to ontological form" (p. L6), and elsewhere, "Seeing-as is the result of the natural attunement of our capacities for perception to the world. In understanding (in seeing-as, in the experience of meaning) we show human thinking's fit with being" (p. L26). This aspect has not been adequately addressed thus far in a cognitive tools approach. Accordingly, I would like to devote the remainder of this chapter to exploring the pedagogical significance of metaphor in evoking ontological sensitivity to particularity (which is, incidentally one of the cognitive tools of "ironic understanding" [Egan, 1997]) or "*this*ness" with, as is the case, birds.

ঀ

> Ontological attention is a response to particularity: *this* porch, *this* laundry basket, *this* day. Its object cannot be substituted for, even when it is an object of considerable generality ('the country', 'cheese', 'garage sales'). It is the antithesis of the attitude that regards things as 'resources', mere means to human ends. In perceiving *this*ness, we respond to having been addressed. (In fact we are addressed all the time, but we don't always notice this.) (Zwicky, 2003, p. L52)

There is a subtle yet troubling ontological shallowness in the following statement by John Gatta: "To read birds, for example, requires familiarity with the articulated sounds of each species. Learning to look with understanding at what is already 'before you' in the text, field, or sandbank is essentially, then, a problem of hermeneutics" (2004, p. 137). Undoubtedly, reading birds involves some sense of familiarity with the sonic expressions of different species (in a taxonomic or epistemological sense, some ornithological knowledge is required to read birds), but ecohermeneutically speaking it also requires finding the attitude (or being taught to find the attitude) to *be read by* or to think *with* a particular bird-being by attending to the exquisite uniqueness of each and every encounter. Reading birds ecohermeneutically entails more than familiarizing oneself with specific sound vibrations as they travel through space and categorizing them as such or drawing on the interdisciplinary learning opportunities presented by "hummingbirds." It calls for hearing "the question" (in this case, *this* bird) properly, for ethical recognition of alterity, attunement to the possibility of kinship, and, one might hope, the responsibility that ensues from learning to love the world vis-à-vis *this* blackbird or thrush.

> It is by a complementary shift of attention that one may suddenly come to hear the familiar song of a blackbird or a thrush in a surprisingly new manner—not just as a pleasant melody repeated mechanically, as on a tape player in the background, but as active meaningful speech. Suddenly, subtle variations in the tone and rhythm of that whistling phrase seem laden with expressive intention, and the two birds singing to each other across the field appear for the first time as attentive, conscious beings, earnestly engaged in the same world that we ourselves engage, yet from an astonishingly different angle and perspective. (Abram, 1996, p. 81)

It is important to reiterate that the experience itself is not "metaphorical." The role of metaphor in ecopoetic thought is not to generate clever new witticisms or expressive descriptions about the world or our experience of it (though this may be a byproduct of this kind of thinking), rather metaphor provides an attentive means of attunement often imployed in conjunction with or as a trace of the immediacy of address (standing, perhaps, with some students in a field and suddenly hearing the familiar sound of a thrush, but this time as a stranger coming home). Or as a trace of such a gesture in text.

ॐ

Being that you and I cannot stand together in a field (unless you take this book with you, go now!), perhaps the following lyrical excerpt from poet, educator and avid birdwatcher Don McKay will help illustrate "the trace" of an ecopoetic encounter. In this case, McKay has turned his attention to bushtits and the profound teachings they can elicit (reminding us first that, for the ancient Chinese, the heart was an organ of thought):

> To be next door to nothing: it's not only their nests, but the bushtits themselves that convey this paradoxical power. They are "creatures of the air" not only because they fly through it, but because it comprises so much of their bodily presence. All birds, in fact, live close to the edge. Typically, they draw air into sacs throughout their bodies, and even, in some cases, into their hollow bones. They also expel all the air from the lungs with each exhalation, without holding back, as we do, a reserve. Nor do they put on fat they aren't about to burn up in migration. Birds do not need a Lao-tzu to remind them of the non-being their lives depend on. (2002, pp. 74-75)

This profound account of thinking with bushtits is a good example of taking up the teachings and giving the text (i.e., the lesson) forms with which our bodies, minds, and memories can really interact (Bringhurst, 2006).

Chapter Four

Metaphor is one of the ways the "wild, participatory logic of the weblike perceptual world" (Abram, 1996, p. 84) resonates in human thought and its thrum can deliquesce the laborious maintenance of a hypostatized attitude of certainty. It is difficult work to think critically, but it also laborious to maintain epistemic certainty and inertia in the face of manifold anomalies and moving experiences of meaning. American poet Louise Gluck has claimed that the role of metaphor is not one of a standardized service (i.e., it is not strictly speaking, *only* a tool for thinking or cognitive development): "Its service is to the spirit, from which it removes the misery of inertia. It does this by refocusing an existing image of the world..." (as cited in Zwicky, 2003, p. L8). The ecological crisis is, in part, exacerbated by a persistent image of the world, a monolithic and essentialized image with aggressive proselytizing tendencies. One of the potential powers of metaphor is its ability to rethink images over and above our wanting and doing and thus remove from us the miserablism of inertia, certainty and inevitability. Although this will certainly involve a good deal of *knowledge*, the point here is that more knowledge, even interdisciplinary knowledge, is not necessarily what is called for. What is more pressing is a reorientation to knowing, a new kind of ontological engagement.

When we think intensely and beautifully, *something happens.*

ৡ

A quick story about thinking with birds: I imagine Rachel Carson (2002) listening to birds, or rather, attuning to the heartbreaking absence of their songs. Ten years after an increase in the use of synthetic pesticides sanctioned by the United States Department of Agriculture in the 1950s, Carson was bedridden from duodenal ulcers and had discovered cysts in her left breast just as she was completing the drafts of a chapter on cancer for her book on the deadly effects of pesticides. The cancer metastasized and reached languidly for her liver. Under the weight of fierce criticism from powerful corporations such as DuPont and their ticker-tape parade of lobbyists, payroll scientists and politicians—and the very real possibility of being sued for libel—she published *Silent Spring* while still undergoing radiation treatment. It was difficult to decide on that title for the book. *Silent Spring* was originally just the title for a chapter on birds, but Carson agreed that it should become a metaphoric title for the entire work, drawing attention to a bleak future for the whole natural world should we continue down this path (Lear, 1997). *Silent Spring* became a watershed for environmental consciousness in North America.

> Although weakened by her treatment
> & the sadness in her left breast
> in the end, Rachel Carson
> died of a heart-attack.

A year after her death, her publisher arranged for the publication of a narrative essay (intended to be a book), entitled *The Sense of Wonder* (Carson, 1965), about her adventures in "nature" with her nephew. More importantly, however, the book was an educational entreaty about the significance of maintaining wonder. In that book she writes:

> Hearing can be a source of even more exquisite pleasure but it requires conscious cultivation. I have had people tell me that they had never heard the song of a wood thrush, although I knew the bell-like phrases of this bird had been ringing in their backyards every spring.... Take time to listen and talk about the voices of the earth and what they mean—the majestic voice of thunder, the winds, the sound of surf or flowing streams.
>
> And the voices of living things: No child should grow up unaware of the dawn chorus of the birds in spring. He will never forget the experience of a specially planned early rising and going out in the predawn darkness. The first voices are heard before daybreak. It is easy to pick out these first, solitary singers. Perhaps a few cardinals are uttering their clear, rising whistles, like someone calling a dog. Then the song of a whitethroat, pure and ethereal, with the dreamy quality of remembered joy. Off in some distant patch of woods a whippoorwill continues his monotonous night chant, rhythmic and insistent, sound that is felt almost more than heard. Robins, thrushes, song sparrows, jays, vireos add their voices. The chorus picks up volume as more and more robins join in, contributing a fierce rhythm of their own that soon becomes dominant in the wild medley of voices. In that dawn chorus one hears the throb of life itself. (pp. 68-69)

Hearing requires conscious cultivation. Not all of us are fortunate enough to have a conservationist like Rachel Carson in the family (or a bird-loving nature poet for that matter) willing to venture out into the predawn darkness to develop the disposition to recognize the "throb of life." Be that as it may, educators are uniquely well positioned to provide, provoke and reflect upon these experiences with their students (or, at least, their trace in texts). And yet students can, and in my experience often do, venture into the "natural world" and never really hear the birdsong in the background or notice the tiny bell-shaped fungi underfoot.

Regrettably, the throb of life in many places has been subdued by the hubbub of anthropic hubris, and this monotonous din can follow us well down the forest path. Metaphoric thinking is one of the educator's most powerful means of drawing students out of our our-centeredness, and educators would be wise to ask what kind of space and opportunity is really provided to "take time to listen and talk about the voices of the earth and what they mean." Rachel Carson *really* listened to birds.

ৡ

Drawing upon the power of metaphoric thinking to critically examine ontological presuppositions and acknowledge, mourn and celebrate our kinship with things is a vital practice for educators to develop in a time of ecological emergency. As part of a pedagogic strategy it joins with other key features of a critical ecohermeneutic approach, some of which I would like to briefly introduce here in order to get a sense of the broader curriculum and where we are heading. Andrejs Kulnieks, Dan Roronhiake:wen Longboat, and Kelly Young are among the few educational theorists to explicitly describe their project as an "eco-hermeneutic approach to learning" (2010). Their understanding of ecohermeneutics builds upon previous inquiries into hermeneutics, oral traditions and environmental education (Kulnieks, 2008; Young, 2007), the work of other hermeneutic researchers in the field (D. Smith, 1991, 2003), and Indigenous knowledge holders who use the land as a primary resource for understanding. Longboat, for example, is a Mohawk scholar from the Six Nations of the Grand River and is known for bringing traditional Haudenosaunee knowledge to bear on environmental education (Longboat, 1999; Sheridan & Longboat, 2006). An ecohermeneutic approach, for these scholars, entails the development of curriculum that moves beyond the classroom and beyond Western presuppositions, suggesting that "reading place" is a hermeneutic task befitting of ecological education. The key features of this curriculum include: engendering a deep and participatory understanding of place; recognizing and revitalizing oral traditions; focusing on interpretive and experiential inquiry with an emphasis on storytelling; and connecting to ecojustice frameworks to analyze the linguistic dimension of the ecological crisis (this approach will be further discussed in chapter eight).

Unlike the Western intellectual tradition, which requires meaning to be linguistic and relies primarily upon textual convention (including philosophical hermeneutics, a theme explored in greater detail in the following chapters), oral and Indigenous traditions have more of a cultural precedent for recognizing more-than-human meaning by, for example, "walking the land" with Elders or storytellers. This is not to say that attending to the land is an innate and native capacity of the body that will simply emerge from being out and about; the Elder or storyteller carefully employs the methodologies of oral traditions (myth, metaphor, rhythm, etc.) as a pedagogical means of drawing attention towards the earth and other beings (Kulnieks et al., 2010, p. 17). In conjunction with the ecophenomenological work of Abram (1996) and the ecopoetic work of Bringhurst (2002), an ecohermeneutic approach suggests that the orature of Indigenous knowledges offers a way to integrate and synthesize more-than-human meaning. This is not to suggest that we abandon writing to "go back" to orality (as if that were an option), but rather that we understand the literary tradition as being part of an oral tradition and recognize both the pedagogical and ecological merits of oral ways of thinking.

> Ecological hermeneutics requires the orature of Indigenous knowledge (IK) precisely because IK works on the ability of the teller to integrate and synthesize knowledge that provides an ecological and temporal location vis-à-vis the natural world. From those constituents, the story is told not as a static text but dynamic meaning derived from the restless and changing energies of the Earth and her dynamics in human form with a transaction of the ecology of meaning. Here we do not mean that there is no right or wrong meanings. That is left to the listener. Rather, there is a methodology for interaction and the unification of mind with place for the realization of the lesson that place has to teach. (Kulnieks et al., 2010, p. 17)

Weaving hermeneutics with Indigenous epistemologies and an ecojustice framework to "re-indigenize" curriculum is a fascinating project and one that, I believe, provides a rich foundation for ecological education. One is tempted to say something like the only prescribed learning outcome of an ecohermeneutic curriculum is to *re-indigenize* thinking, such that it becomes calibrated with the places we are *of*. But how is one to claim this without reproducing colonial logics? Especially being that as I write these words I occupy unceded Coast Salish territory in a colonial state that has used its education system, both historically and contemporarily, to perpetuate genocide against the Indigenous peoples of this land (Alfred, 1999; Battiste, 2013; Cardinal, 1969; Maracle, 1996). Admittedly, when I began working on an ecological reading of philosophical hermeneutics I did not necessarily foresee having to address some of the complex issues of Indigeneity and colonial politics, but within Canada, and particularly here in "British Columbia," one cannot think ecohermeneutically without addressing colonization. We will never make a home here (i.e., enact *ecopoïesis*) if we do not address—with humility, bowing low to the humus of our history and being—the colonial logics of the education system and reshape it to work towards the revitalization of Indigenous peoples, lands and lifestyles. As we will see (chapter eight), ecohermeneutic "re-indigenization" must entail decolonization, which is to say, it must engender "ethical relationality" between Indigenous and non-Indigenous peoples (Donald, 2009).

Before we delve any further into the complexities of braiding ecohermeneutics with Indigenous epistemologies, however, I would like to first explore some of the Western substrates in which the hermeneutic tradition emerged. The next three chapters will be devoted to a brief ecoexegesis of some of the key European thinkers of this tradition, namely Martin Heidegger and Hans-Georg Gadamer (and very briefly, Paul Ricoeur). As we will see, the hermeneutic tradition itself is not without its own anthropocentric prejudices. One of the objectives of ecohermeneutic recycling is to mycoremediate some of these hypostatized epistemicides, but more importantly it is a means, I hope, of revitalizing the hermeneutic tradition and bringing its wisdom to bear on our lives as they are lived (in a time when we are in desperate need of such wisdom). There is something vitally important in the hermeneutic habit of returning to the history and ancestry of things to look again for signs of life amongst the decay. Here, walking a boreal forest path with a group of students, for example, the leaves of these old books strike us as significant in new ways and call us to new questions.

chapter five

inoculating hermeneutics: Heidegger substrates

> A hermeneutic interest in tradition and ancestry (an interest in what Gary Snyder called "the old ways") requires not simply the protective repetition of such traditions. Hermeneutics incites the particularities and intimacies of our lives to call these traditions to account, compelling them to bear witness to the lives we are living. Hermeneutics demands of such disciplines and traditions that they tell us what they know about keeping the world open and enticing and alive and inviting. And, to the extent that such disciplines and traditions can no longer serve this deeply pedagogical purpose, to that extent they are no longer telling, no longer helpful in our living, no longer true. (Jardine, 1998, p. 2)

Before we consider any specific features of an ecohermeneutic curriculum, I would like to ground this work in the modern hermeneutic tradition via a brief engagement with two of its foundational philosophers: Martin Heidegger (1962, 2001) and Hans-Georg Gadamer (2013). Their philosophical orientations, strategies and some of their key hermeneutic concepts will provide the substrates[1] whereby we can inoculate and rethink these philosophers in light of more recent environmental theory and from within a world faced with ecological emergency. Ecohermeneutic inoculation in this respect is a deliquescent move—at once critical and remedial—that compels a tradition to reveal what it knows, what it has yet to teach, and where it needs to reconnect in order to remain in resonance with the world and our lives as they are now lived. In this sense, an

---

1   The materials inoculated with spores and upon which mycelia and mushrooms are grown are called "substrates" by mushroom growers (Stamets, 2005, p. 126).

ecohermeneutic imagination is less interested with ontological questioning that pursues metaphysical Truth and, by extension, with Heidegger as a philosopher of the Truth of Being. Rather what we are concerned with here is "salvaging" and revitalizing these philosophic substrates to bring them to bear on ecological pedagogy in a more-than-human world.

As environmental scholar Kevin Deluca has maintained, this may require us to think with Heidegger "after-philosophy" as it is traditionally conceived, which will entail neither straightforward textual exegesis nor critique per se, but reading Heidegger for social and political efficacy as "equipment for living in the world on earth." (2005, p. 70) While I remain a little apprehensive about "equipment" metaphors, Deluca's proposition does provide a compelling means to move beyond archaic strivings for a foundational and totalizing ontology towards ontological inquiry as a *way of thinking*. This is an important reflexive capacity to hone even as we turn our attention towards hermeneutics itself, which does not descend to us from the pure vacuum of transcendental space but emerges from the presupposition-laden humus of particular times, places and traditions.

Philosophical hermeneutics has long positioned itself in opposition to the Enlightenment projects of objectivity, instrumental rationality and univocal essentialism. Its anti-Cartesian roots reach back to the beginnings of "modernity" with the writings of Baruch Spinoza and Giambattista Vico, and continue through to Romantic hermeneutic philosophers such as Friedrich Schleiermacher and Wilhelm Dilthey (for a brief historical overview see D. Smith, 1999; also see Mueller-Vollmer, 1994). Yet having emerged from the modernist European milieu in a world of proto-ecological awareness, the tradition conceals presuppositions that distort its resonance with contemporary life. Inoculation thus aims to mycoremediate the tradition itself; to deliquesce the toxic hypostatized residuum buried within, and open the hermeneutic landscape for new generations, connections with new fields and new insights from traditional fields, and to prepare the ground for new forms of life to flourish.

Although the hermeneutic phenomenology of the twentieth century, the ontological and linguistic turns beginning with Heidegger and Gadamer, are particularly fecund substrates, Gadamer's "linguisticality of understanding," for example, will require ecoexegesis in order to reach beyond the horizon of human exceptionalism (a theme explored in chapter six). Likewise, there is much in the work of Heidegger that we might bring to bear on education in a more-than-human world. In this chapter I will offer a brief ecoexegesis of three aspects of Heideggerian thought: the historicity of understanding, the significance of ontological inquiry, and the way technological enframing limits our relational possibilities. In rejecting strict piety to textual exegesis, as Deluca has suggested, I hope we can at once pay respect to, and move beyond, Heideggerian hermeneutics towards an ecohermeneutic sensibility concerned with more ecologically just ways of learning and living (2005, p. 68).

The literature by and about Heidegger is superabundant. He is undeniably one of the most eminent (and troublesome) philosophers of the twentieth century. As such, he serves as the springboard for a legion of philosophic discourses, particularly those concerned with environmental ethics as he was one of the only "first rank" philosophical figures to address the devastation of the earth (Heidegger, 1962, 1977, 1993, 2001; also see Zimmerman, 1983; Cooper, 2005). While in many respects he remains the go-to philosopher for environmental theory, Deluca has suggested that Heidegger is most commonly cited in this literature not to develop a more robust theory but to lend "borrowed legitimacy" to the whole "fledgling enterprise" (2005, p. 68). This is not to claim that Heidegger ought to be abandoned (or environmental theory for that matter), but rather his thinking should be called to bear witness to the particularities, intimacies and the sufferings of being in a world of ecological crisis. This also does not imply we simply greenwash Heidegger and appropriate his thought wholesale; he was, after all, the first Nazi Rector of the University of Freiburg, and there is a troubling political defeatism inherent in his sense that the logic of machination is inevitable. In spite of his appalling politics and grand metaphysical wont, however, there is an indefatigable sense that Heidegger may yet have something to offer. Environmental responses to Heidegger have tended to fall roughly into two categories: Heidegger as proto-environmentalist (Evernden, 1993, pp. 79–105) or Heidegger as Nazi and, by association, radical environmentalism and non-anthropocentric thought as suspiciously fascist (Deluca, 2005, pp. 68–69). An ecoexegesis will, one hopes, avoid falling into these prescribed categories by remaining appropriately critical and yet open to imploying Heidegger as "equipment," or rather, as a viable substrate that can be brought to bear on ecological education as a project aimed at cultural transformation.

Despite the tendency for impassioned reactions to Heidegger, there can be no doubt that his philosophy is the yield of a man who deeply contemplated human-world relations. It is interesting to note, while clearly involved in teaching for most of his life, he rarely refers directly to pedagogy. Still, because much of his writing is so concerned with the ontological dimension of human-world relation, I share in the sense that his thinking could have profound implications

Chapter Five

for ecological pedagogy (Bonnett, 2002). His philosophical oeuvre is, of course, much too broad to address in any depth here, but let's begin with some of his key hermeneutic insights as a means of beginning to think ecohermeneutically with Heidegger.

ૡ

Writing from the field of nursing, Tina Koch (1995) has produced a condensed summary of some of the essential notions of Heideggerian hermeneutics (in comparison to Husserlian phenomenology) that may be useful in providing a basic overview. The fundamental notion I want to consider is the significance of the *historicity of understanding*, which is related to three additional, but interrelated concepts:

> *Background* is handed down to a person at birth from their culture and presents a way of understanding the world. This understanding determines what is "real" for the individual and as such, Heidegger assumes that background meanings, skills and practices cannot be made *completely* explicit (in response to Husserlian "bracketing"). Much of the hermeneutic task is bringing these presuppositions to the foreground.
>
> *Pre-understanding* refers to the meanings and organizations of a culture (including language and practices) which are already in the world before we understand. Human beings always approach a situation with a pre-understanding. These stories are always already part of a shared background and are hermeneutically brought into focus in order to be interpreted and critiqued.
>
> *Co-constitution* is a way of understanding the process of person-world co-creation. Co-constitutionality refers to the philosophical assumption of indissoluble unity between person and world. This means being constructed by the world in which we live and at the same time constructing this world from our own experience and agency. A person participates in this a priori world in cultural, historical, and social contexts. (p. 831)

Obviously these concepts are more philosophically sophisticated than can be captured here, but I hope this gives a sense of Heidegger's foundational importance in the ontological turn in hermeneutics. The historicity of understanding lies at the very heart of the hermeneutic project and, broadly speaking, ecohermeneutics is an extension of the ontological turn applied to the significance that historicity bears upon earthly being-in-the-world. For the purposes of this chapter, I will briefly touch upon each of the related concepts and offer an ecoexegetical reading to underline how ecological understanding is either absent or marginalized and how these Heideggerian notions might be reconnected to environmental theory to incorporate more-than-human otherness.

Being that more and more people today are born (or forced) into highly urbanized, media saturated, and profoundly human-shaped environments (and more of the earth is rendered to this end), the concept of *background* is particularly interesting from an ecological perspective. Not only are "moderns" born into a cultural background with a preexistent membrane or matrix of anthropocentric prejudice between self and "world" (referring here more to "lifeworld" or being-in-the-world), but there is a kind of thickening effect with the advent of late industrial life that reduces reciprocal exchange and further estranges people from the immediacy of the "natural world" as an agential *world-on-its-own-terms*. The effects of living and thinking within a dense anthropic bubble on what we consider "real" and worthy of axiological consideration are significant. The sensuous dimensions of experience, the architecture, the very structure of urbanized places emanates a cacophony of anthropos so vociferous it essentially drowns out most or all "naturally occurring" more-than-human presence(s). While we must, on a certain level, contend with the prevailing global drift (or rather capitalist thrust) towards urbanization, the ecohermeneutic educator must also remain vigilant and critically question the way in which *human* backgrounds *more-than-human*, lest we forfeit environmental design and possibility to neoliberal architects (for a related discussion as it pertains to urban environmental education see Derby, Piersol & Blenkinsop, 2015).

The work of ecofeminist Val Plumwood (1993) also provides a fascinating way to rethink background from an ecological perspective, both deepening the critique of a Cartesian ontology[2] and offering a potential pedagogic strategy to deliquesce the dualistic boundary between human and world. Plumwood describes parallels between the instrumentalization of nature and women, claiming that both become the "background" against which the dominant and historically recognized subjects perform (i.e., male / female, reason / nature, subject / object). She explains:

> This backgrounding of women and nature is deeply embedded in the rationality of the economic system and in the structures of contemporary society. What is involved in the backgrounding of nature is the denial of dependence on biospheric processes, and

---

2   This is not to claim that Plumwood's project is in any way an extension of Heideggerian hermeneutics, only that they share in a critique of Cartesian dualism and the rationalist tradition.

a view of humans as apart, outside of nature, which is treated as a limitless provider without needs of its own. (p. 21)

As we have seen in previous chapters, this backgrounding of more-than-human subjectivity is one of the most pressing concerns for ecological educators. How are we to learn how to listen to the world if we are culturally inculcated not to recognize its voice(s)—that the world has needs, perspectives and designs of its own beyond our wanting and doing? If the task of Heideggerian hermeneutics is bringing the historical composition of the world to the foreground, the task of critical ecohermeneutics is bringing the (historically effected) interrelational composition of more-than-human interbeing to the foreground. Again this suggests that ecocritical analysis of the dominant culture's human-world presuppositions is an important aspect of this work, but that we must equally strive to make free spaces whereby the more-than-human is foregrounded and afforded a political and pedagogical voice for itself.

With respect to *pre-understanding*, ecohermeneutics shares in the Heideggerian notion that cultural stories, language use and social practices must be brought into focus to understand our being-in-the-world. The critical task here entails discerning what calls for this kind of inquiry in a world of ecological crisis? What historically bequeathed pre-understandings leach the humus of earthly being-in-the-world? How are these presuppositions embedded in the practices, environments and structures of the conventional education experience? How might we move from using language to critically reflect on cultural pre-understandings to imploying it to listen to the polyphony of interbeing? As we have seen, an ecohermeneutic response is to analyze the root metaphors of our ecological estrangement as well as draw upon the lyric capacity of metaphor (amongst other contemplative practices and oral methodologies) to draw students towards more attentive and resonant relation with things. This move, although ontologically motivated, takes us well beyond Heidegger's central concerns with Truth and Being and into the realms of environmental ethics, politics, social theory, and, of course, education. Despite these metaphysically sacrilegious moves, the essence of a Heideggerian approach remains intact: ontological questioning as a *way of thinking* (a theme we will explore later in this chapter).

Co-constitutionality is perhaps the most interesting Heideggerian notion from an ecological perspective. The concept originally draws from the assumption of an indissoluble unity between person and world, acknowledging that a person participates in cultural, historical and social contexts, but one will note, despite the use of the word "world," the absence of an "ecological" context. This is, of course, largely the result of Heideggerian hermeneutics arising from a particular cultural situation in which ecological concerns were either nonexistent or nascent. When Heidegger uses the word "world," he means, something like the preexisting and essentially human "cultural-historical world" that we already find ourselves in before we begin reflecting upon it. An ecohermeneutic rendering works to deepen this concept to include the interrelated and agential more-than-human ecology in which we are also always already immersed in and constituted of. Perhaps "eco-constitutionality" is a term that might remind us that our being is always *housed*.

Eco-constitutionality seems closer to what French phenomenologist Maurice Merleau-Ponty referred to as "flesh." In his later work, Merleau-Ponty (1969) writes less about "the body" and begins to write instead about the collective "flesh," which signifies both *our flesh* and *the flesh of the world*. As Abram explains, Merleau-Ponty attempts to describe here an elemental power that has no name in Western philosophy:

> The Flesh is the mysterious tissue or matrix that underlies and gives rise to both the perceiver and the perceived as interdependent aspects of its own spontaneous activity. It is the reciprocal presence of the sentient in the sensible and of the sensible in the sentient, a mystery of which we have always, at least tacitly, been aware, since we have never been able to affirm one of these phenomena, the perceivable world or the perceiving self, without implicitly affirming the existence of the other...the perceiving being and the perceived being are of the same *stuff*, the perceiver and the perceived are interdependent and in some sense even reversible aspects of a common animate element, or Flesh, that is *at once both sensible and sensitive*. (1996, pp. 66-67)

An ecohermeneutic rendering of co-constitutionality, it seems to me, could be understood in similar terms: an animate, agential and reciprocal matrix of interdependence all the way down. In this sense, eco-constitutionality forms the elemental, yet historically effected, substratum from which cultural pre-understandings emerge and respond to. In his treatment of the late works of Edmund Husserl, Abram underlines the importance of the earth for all human cognition in the phenomenological tradition calling it the "secret depth of the life-world" and, in the words of Husserl himself, this earthly matrix is the "root basis" of our experience (1996, p. 43). A person is still understood to participate a priori in a world of cultural, historical, and social contexts, but also beneath these dimensions there is participatory reciprocity with a vibrant ecology that sustains, shapes and comprises all things. Our flesh is thus the flesh of the world, not simply the subjectivized flesh of individual embodiment.

A Cartesian ontology, on the other hand, emerges from a reductionist human-world relation that implies people are detached subjects utilizing inanimate matter, which has profound ethical implications:

> Descartes' ontology presumes the dynamic of an isolated subject grasping mathematically world as object. Arguably, it is this perspective that is at the root of the environmental crisis, for the world is reduced to an object laid out before me and I am reduced to a detached subject that has only a use-relation to a dead world. (Deluca, 2005, p. 73)

Heideggerian hermeneutics focuses attention on our implicatedness in historicity; ecohermeneutics cultivates a similar critical-historical sensibility, but also draws attention to our implicatedness in the eco-constitutionality of interbeing (our shared *flesh*). As the following passage illustrates, this move towards earthly being-in-the-world is not all that far from some of Heidegger's own late sentiments about the earth being, "that on which and in which man bases his dwelling in the world.... Upon the earth and in it, historically man grounds his dwelling in the world.... The world grounds itself on the earth, and earth juts through the world" (Heidegger, 1993, pp. 169–172). Pedagogically speaking, the task thus becomes foregrounding cultural pre-understandings to ecocritically analyze our relations and "bringing forth" (i.e., clearing space to allow for an experience of "bringing forth") the more-than-human background. If we were to play with some prepositions and verbs we use to describe human-world relations, a Cartesian perspective might best be described as a *to-relation* (subject *to* object, as in *using*), Heideggerian hermeneutics would be an *in-relation* (being-*in*-the-world, as in *dwelling*), and ecohermeneutics a move towards an *of-relation* or perhaps a *within-relation* (being *of* earth, as in *resonating*).[3]

> Just as we do not speak for the sake of speaking but speak to someone *of* something or *of* someone, and in this initiative of speaking an aiming at the world is involved upon which is suspended all *that which* we say.... The effective, present, ultimate and primary being, the thing itself, are in principle apprehended in transparency through their perspectives, offer themselves therefore only to someone who wishes not to have them but to see them, not to hold them as with forceps, or to immobilize them as under the objective of a microscope, but to let them be and to witness their continued being— to someone who therefore limits himself to giving them the hollow, the free space they

---

3 We might also think about using clusters of prepositions. Descartes (to-at-on-against-over-beyond-versus), Heidegger (in-with-among-along-amidst-during), ecohermeneutics (of-as-from-within-in-between).

ask for in return, the resonance they require, who follows their own movement, who is therefore not a nothingness the full being would come to stop up, but a question consonant with the porous being which it questions and from which it obtains not an *answer*, but a confirmation of its astonishment. (Merleau-Ponty, 1968, pp. 101-102)

ঽ

Let's turn now to Heidegger's strategy of ontological inquiry as a *way of thinking* in ecological education. In his essay, "The Question Concerning Technology" Heidegger writes: "Questioning builds a way. We would be advised, therefore, above all to pay heed to the way and not to fix our attention on isolated sentences and topics. The way is one of thinking" (1993, p. 311). As Deluca suggests, this philosophic strategy read "after-philosophy" models a way of thinking shaped less by metaphysics or utopian "groundplans" and more by a "gift of distress" that impels us down a path of open, honest and, indeed, painful questioning. For what deserves to be called into question in a world of ecological emergency?

> What is crucial here is that Heidegger is offering us the gift of distress if we have the courage to embark on the path of questioning, of mindfulness, that casts into doubt all of our taken-for-granted. Heidegger is not offering us answers or programs or utopian projections. Traveling the path is our task of thinking. (2005, p. 71)

Having the courage to embark down the path is, I believe, the vocational task of calling of ecological educators who must contend with deeply engrained habits and ecologically destructive conventions. In an age of mass distraction and prescribed solutions there is something wild and enlivening about mindfully traveling down the path with no prescriptions in mind and seeing where it takes you no matter what is called into question. There is also something pedagogically significant in the notion of the gift of distress. All too often the anguish, anger and loss that surfaces in environmental discourse are either marginalized or avoided in education. Or if distress does emerge, it tends to be quickly channelled into more "positive" and ostensibly empowering discussions regarding "green solutions" or "ten things you can do to save our planet."

The oscillation between the existential distress required to generate critical distance and the receptivity required for a relational intimacy with things describes the fundamental tension of an ecohermeneutic mind. The first four chapters of this book were, by and large, devoted to lyric thinking and the significance of attending to the phenomenology of marginalized experiences as a means of eliciting affinity and healing (which is not to say sans loss or rage, the critical and remedial are synchronous); now we travel a little further down the sometimes disquieting path of ontological questioning as a way of thinking in education. In order to do this I will draw parallels between the Heidegger-inspired "gift of distress" and Blenkinsop's (2012) exploration of "four slogans" for place-based educational projects aimed at cultural transformation. Blenkinsop's four slogans are as follows:

- Everything is up for grabs
- This is gonna hurt
- Maintain "hyperactive pessimism"
- When in doubt remember the ecosystem

The first slogan has, I believe, already been sufficiently discussed in previous chapters: the idea that the conventional school system, in the modern Western context, is embedded in an ecologically and socially unjust ontology. Thus any attempt to effect change calls for more than superficial adjustments of current practice, it requires an approach based on a radically different ethos. Blenkinsop adds, "A further implication is that everything within a particular cultural milieu has been shaped and coloured by it. This does not imply that everything must necessarily be discarded, but rather that everything deserves scrutiny and reappraisal." (2012, p. 10). Put into Heideggerian terms, we are never isolated subjects who stand back and survey an objective world: "The Interpretation of the world begins, in the first instance, with some entity within-the-world, so that the phenomenon of the world in general no longer comes into view" (1962, p. 122). It is the ubiquity and invisibility of the ecologically destructive habits of the dominant culture (not to mention their enshrinement in many of the educational objectives of present day institutions) that necessitate the gift of distress and the first slogan in educational projects that aim to root them out.

I will address the second and third slogans respectively in the following paragraphs as a means of further exploring the implications of a Heideggerian way of thinking on ecohermeneutic pedagogy. As for the final slogan, I believe it too has already been sufficiently discussed as it describes the essential gesture of an ecohermeneutic sensibility. It could equally be adopted as a slogan for ecohermeneutic pedagogy, maybe even drop the doubt and simply say (as in the ringing of a bell):

remember the ecosystem.

৶

Bringing a Heideggerian way of thinking to bear on ecological education calls upon teachers to take up the role of existential dissonator (Denton, 1972); the one who engenders distress and models the courage required to travel and attend to the way. This role corresponds with Blenkinsop's second slogan: This is gonna hurt.

> Pain occurs at moments of fundamental change because, as we apprehend a new awareness, former deeply held beliefs and behaviours are thrown into question. The ground upon which we have built our lives appears to be less stable and in conflict with this new consciousness. Things we have done in the past are no longer acceptable to us, but not only are our personal histories becoming troublesome, so too is the ecological record of our culture. (2012, p. 21)

It seems unlikely, and realistically undesirable, that any genuine existential insight might emerge without coming to face such potentially painful moments; particularly, in light of the record of the dominant culture. By way of an interesting illustration of this slogan, consider many of the ecologically-minded poets and philosophers we have been discussing—Zwicky, Bringhurst, Lilburn, McKay, Lee, Hirschfield, Abram—whose work consistently orbits a sense of loss and of the "role of penthos in everyday life" (Glenn, 2010, p. 5).[4] Ecological educators in turn would be wise to develop what Joanna Macy and Molly Young Brown have called "despair work" (1998, p. 71). This does not mean dwelling needlessly on suffering and politically paralyzing doomsaying but acknowledging that there is much to mourn and that loss is a part of the fabric of our lives that need not be palliated with green "positivity" and false hope. The gift of distress is the beginning of a path to be traveled, not some defeatist or starry-eyed waypoint to be settled upon. Indeed, it is deemed a *gift* precisely because it removes the misery of such inertia and impels one towards disciplined ontological questioning as an evolving disposition, but due to the discomfort of having our habits and certainties deliquesced, it is likely that a teacher will be required to "build" a way and travel compassionately and mindfully with students (and with one's self) wherever the path leads.

In his reading of the work of Buber for educational theory, Blenkinsop (2005) has claimed that it is up to the educator to both sanction the inherent instinct for communion (with human and more-than-human kin) and provide

---

4   Penthos was the ancient Greek spirit of grief, mourning and lamentation.

Chapter Five

opportunities for it to flourish. This is all the more important during existential moments of insight where there may be ideological emphases in the culture that work to marginalize certain experiences.

> The teacher must always be present, be available and reaching towards the student, proffering relationship, even if the student is uninterested, unwilling or unable to consciously accept it. This is equally as important before the moment of insight as it is thereafter, when the student may begin certain tentative conscious responses. (p. 292)

Blenkinsop continues by outlining how, for the educator engaged in her own journey as well as supporting others down the path, there is a profound need for humility (p. 293). An ecohermeneutic pedagogy does not, like Heidegger, offer answers or utopian projections, traveling the path with humility and a mind drawn towards the humus of our being is the task of thinking.

> We are human, full of *humus*. Truly *human* understanding must have a certain *humility*, a certain aspect of not being the center of everything and the only voice worth heeding. It must reorient to an ongoing conversation with the Earth, a conversation that *must be sustained if life is to go on*. (Jardine, 1998, p. 28)

There is much ado in environmental education these days about avoiding the olde "doom and gloom" tactics of early environmentalists that scared students into depressed passivity with extinction rates or images of deforestation or population projections for future megacities. Although I share in refraining from fear-based scare tactics (ecological education as an anti-smoking campaign), especially when working with younger children, I find some variants of this steadfast optimism steeped in a troublesome denial. In order to speak to this more clearly and continue exploring Heideggerian questioning as a way of thinking, I offer Blenkinsop's third slogan which employs a term borrowed from Michel Foucault's (1984) description of himself as an ongoing and suspicious cultural questioner: Maintain "hyperactive pessimism" (Blenkinsop, 2012, p. 10).

Even from this side of the page I can feel "liberal-minded" educators cringe at the sound of "hyperactive pessimism." They start fumbling through a re-usable shopping bag desperate for their little book of Dalai Lama quotes and raising what ecophilosopher Derrick Jensen has called a "Gandhi shield" (2006, p. 79). "Stay positive, stay positive. Be the change." A Heideggerian way of questioning offers a more sensible and judicious means of responding to the ecological record of the dominant culture and our implicit collusion with its malignant conventions. Surely in a social milieu so utterly steeped in ideology and besieged by the rhetoric of a neoliberal "common-sense" revolution—not to mention enthralled by deeper logics like anthropocentric bias or patriarchy—hyperactive pessimism becomes one of the vocational conditions of being an educator.

> To put it plainly, in environmental circles it is still a Cartesian world, wherein the founding act is human thinking (cogito ergo sum) and the earth is object to humanity's subject. This position is clear in mainstream environmentalism, where humans act to save the object earth and, fundamentally, this action is motivated by the subject's self interest. So, we must save the rain forests because they contain potential medical resources and because they alleviate global warming. (Deluca, 2005, pp. 71-72)

To put it plainly, the environmental educational field is *also* predominantly Cartesian. There is something essential in responding to this greenwashed surface reality with the tenacity of a hyperactive cultural critic. Foucault's "pessimism" is not meant to provoke either wallowing in political paralysis or responding to current events with resolute positivity, rather it is the sobering realization that seismic change is not so easily achieved and a vigilant suspicion is required to inoculate the deep superstructure of our worldview (Blenkinsop, 2012, p. 13). A hermeneutics of suspicion is all the more necessary in education where we stand paradoxically at the generation and reproduction, but also the potential decay and revitalization of cultural habit. Immersed as we are in a matrix of cultural signs, we require a certain amount of distress and suspicion in order to, as Blenkinsop has maintained, "see how this metaphor of 'school' carries with it the epistemology, ontology, and axiology of the culture. How lurking in every locker, from the number and lock on the front to the textbooks and gym shoes inside, are confirmations of a particular worldview" (p. 12).

Be that as it may, sweeping suspicion in education can only take us so far (or rather it may invariably lead to the same chasm on the path: a totalizing negation of everything). How might we continue to walk an indeterminate but ethically-minded path as hyperactive pessimists avoiding both the desire to settle with some hypostatized Truth or the threat of falling into a fissure of total epistemic skepticism? In order to navigate this impasse I invoke Egan's notion of "ironic understanding" as one of the objectives of educational development. As we will see, an educated mind for Egan is one that is capable of the kind of radical epistemic doubt we would expect from a hyperactive pessimist, but also a sophisticated reflexivity that allows for simultaneous, multivocal understandings based on the particularities of a situation. In order to provide context for the

Chapter Five

development of "ironic understanding" I will briefly revisit a cognitive tools approach to education as articulated by the Imaginative Education Research Group.

ॐ

The collective body of theories and practices known as Imaginative Education (Egan, 1997; 2005; Egan & Madej, 2010; Judson, 2010; Gajdamaschko, 2005; Blenkinsop, 2009; Fettes, 2010; Waddington & Johnson, 2010) represent a unique approach to learning that centralizes emotional and imaginative engagement in the learning process and differs significantly from conventional pedagogy in two principal ways. The first being that imagination constitutes the heart and dynamic of all learning, and the second, that learning is a culturally mediated activity. While the first principle is a profoundly fascinating topic (see Egan, 1997; Egan & Nadaner, 1988; Greene, 1995; Jardine, 1998) and, in a sense, also lies at the heart of an ecohermeneutic approach to pedagogy, I will focus on the second principle as a way to continue exploring how a Heidegger-inspired way of ontological questioning might inform ecological education.

According to Egan (1997), an *educated mind* is one that is fully equipped and practiced with the cultural-based strategies or "tools" with which humans make sense of the world. An Imaginative Education thus aims to develop these cognitive tools and, by extension, develop as fully as possible the different "kinds of understanding" these tools enable. As previously mentioned (in chapter four), a cognitive tools approach finds much overlap with the work of Vygotsky (1978, 1986, 2004), who proposed that higher psychological processes are developed vis-à-vis the internalization of different features of one's cultural environment (especially different aspects of language use). These cultural-linguistic aspects of our learning are "mediating tools" that, in turn, profoundly influence the kind of sense one makes of the world. By way of illustration, Judson points to metaphor as an example:

> This cognitive tool has already helped both you and me to make sense of the notion of the cognitive tool. The notion of "tool" leads us to think, perhaps, of a gardening tool or some other kind of implement that helps us to do something. A gardening tool helps us to garden; a building tool helps us to build. A "cognitive" tool, by metaphoric extension, helps us to think. Metaphor is a cognitive tool that, by representing something (a feature of language) as something else (a tool), offers insights and meanings that can deepen understanding. (2010, pp. 36–37)

As we internalize cognitive tools and transition between kinds of understanding, the nature of our emotional and intellectual engagement with the world reorients dramatically. Egan (1997) describes five kinds of understanding to represent how the mind "makes sense" when employing particular cognitive tools: somatic, mythic, romantic, philosophic, and ironic. These kinds of understandings should not be thought of as innate developmental or hierarchical "stages" of learning (contra Piagetian models of psychological development); rather, the development of different kinds of understanding emerges from contexts that employ, enable and enrich their associated cognitive toolkits. In other words, while we may acquire basic potential "forms" of cognitive tools by virtue of having a body or using oral language, in order to sophisticate these tools and deepen our understanding we require educative activities (Judson, 2010, p. 38).

One of the key insights of Imaginative Education is the acknowledgment that each new kind of understanding entails "gains and losses." Kinds of understanding do not represent a linear progression towards a superior form of thinking, rather the development of each new kind of understanding invariably entails the loss or impoverishment of certain ways of sense-making characterized by "previous" kinds of engagement (Judson, 2010). Furthermore, it is one's cultural context and background, to a certain extent, that determines the appropriateness or axiological significance of each kind of understanding. While the transition between each kind of understanding is a compelling topic (Egan, 1997), I will focus primarily on the threat posed by "philosophic understanding"—ways of making sense that derive from the drive for generality, hypothesis and experimentation, and the search for authority and truth—that become too rigidly vested in these generalized constructs as essential Truth. Egan's response to this potential for epistemic hypostatization is to conceive of philosophic understanding as enfolded into ironic understanding—an engagement that results from a deliquescent-like "breakdown or decay of general schemes" (Egan, 1997, p. 138). I contend that the ability and discipline to move between philosophic and ironic understanding, the fruitful composition of bodies of knowledge and their ironic deliquescence, provide a sophisticated means of enacting hyperactive pessimism in education.

Although Egan does not explicitly address ecological issues in any substantive way, his ideas have attracted the attention and consideration of many ecologically-minded educational theorists (Judson, 2010; Fettes & Judson, 2011; Blenkinsop, 2009; Blenkinsop & Fettes, 2009; Fettes, 2011, 2012). I would like to reinforce these connections by bringing Egan's notion of the pedagogical significance of irony to bear on ecohermeneutic pedagogy. Although irony is notoriously multifaceted and difficult to characterize, Egan has aptly identified irony, and the form of consciousness associated with it, as "the master trope of our age" (although its inception was cotemporaneous with the birth of Western civilization itself) (1997, p. 140). Egan has defined an ironic kind of understanding as the "culmination" of an educated mind derived from the development of cognitive tools such as radical epistemic doubt, reflexivity, and the ability to coalesce and integrate multivocal understandings in particular contexts (1997, pp. 137-162).

Egan's historical analysis of ironic understanding invokes its Socratic origins and traces its maturation by way of such eminent modern thinkers as Hegel, Kierkegaard and Nietzsche. He is insistent upon the notion of ironic understanding as a sophisticated ability to negate systems of knowing, not, as it is sometimes made out to be, a shallow manifestation of sarcasm or skill with the ironic features of language (p. 142). The power and relevance of this so-called *negative irony* cannot be understated, for although it is associated with Socrates, Plato and the ancient tradition of epistemic skepticism, it is equally associated with a kind of psychological freedom that few modern ironists would sacrifice for the illusory securities of conventional thought. As Egan has maintained, "If nothing else, it signals knowledge of the unreliability of words and declares a kind of freedom. This freedom may not make one as cheerful as Socrates, but it is not insignificant" (p. 144).

Interestingly, Egan describes ironic ability as based in the resolution between the identity of poetry and thinking, pointing to one of the fundamental insights of uber-ironist Nietzsche: "Nietzsche resolves the ancient quarrel between philosophy and poetry by pointing out that philosophy is no less fictive than is poetry. We are to discard the old distinctions between fiction and truth and recognize rather that there are two kinds of fiction: one that masquerades as truth and one that recognizes itself as fiction" (p. 150). The danger posed by privileging the kinds of metanarratives and general schemes typical of philosophical understanding is that they can come to masquerade as the Truth and transmogrify into some variant of fundamentalism, foundationalism, essentialism, scientism or whatever name is most fashionable for univocal ontologic authority. And as we have seen, ontological rigidity, such as that exemplified by Cartesianism, can bear grave ecological consequences. Negative irony plays a vital role here in decaying and negating the monolithic structures of univocal certainty and to the extent that the hyperactive pessimist requires negative irony to seed (or rather, spore) radical epistemic doubt, it is a necessary feature of being an educator in these times. But again, what of the problem of total negation? How might we conceive of a more sophisticated irony in order to continue down the path of questioning whilst remaining open to the validity, utility and resonant beauty of particular strategies in particular circumstances?

Sophisticated irony, as Egan understands it, differs from its negative counterpart in that it succeeds in achieving reflexiveness without suppressing or utterly negating other kinds of understanding. Rather than doubting every perspective, it seeks to recognize the limited validity in all perspectives, "to believe all metanarratives, to accept all epistemological schemes, to give assent to every belief" (1997, pp. 161–162). A sophisticated ironic understanding thus seeks to avoid the potential of a totalizing negative irony; which is to say, collapsing everything is itself a static kind of engagement with the world. The fluent ironist develops an ability to slip from perspective to perspective, recognizing the merits and limits of each and, more importantly, instilling doubt about the security of what is seen from any one kind of understanding in isolation from others. A sophisticated sense of irony informed by ecohermeneutics would maintain the importance of developing radical epistemic doubt while remaining open to the possibility, for example, that the Enlightenment project may not be hopelessly exhausted; or that the empirical sciences may yet come into resonance with a more-than-human kinship; or that even a former Nazi and grand metaphysician might yet provide useful substrates for ecological flourishing. Mushrooms blooming from the decay.

Egan has written, "What I want to retain in ironic understanding is the corrosion not only of the belief that general schemes reflect the truth about reality but also of the belief that they cannot. That is, Ironic understanding avoids commitment to the incredulity common in postmodernism.... Ironic understanding embraces the irony of postmodernism but not its dismissive certainties..." (1997, p. 156). This speaks volumes to an ecohermeneutic vision of hyperactive pessimism as an educative practice. We require educators who are able to draw students imaginatively towards the explanatory power and emotional satisfaction of generalized theory and metanarratives, while provoking them to resist the belief that truth somehow resides in those constructs rather than being housed within a multivocal world (although Egan does not "go ecological" with this, here I mean both a multivocal life-world and a polyphonic, multispecies more-than-human world).

> This openness to possibility is not credulity or simple-mindedness but, rather, the result of a flexible, buoyant recognition of a multivocal world, within and without...the

sophisticated ironist enjoys an abundant consciousness of varied ways of understanding, and can appreciate a varied spectrum of perspectives while concluding that some are better or more valid or more helpful or more beautiful than others in particular circumstances and for particular purposes. (1997, p. 162)

Egan's interests lie with what language and imagination can do for us in education and are focused primarily on questions of epistemology. While ironic understanding provides an interesting means to think about employing the gift of distress in education and developing a sophisticated and reflexive hyperactive pessimism, I want to continue walking a little farther down the path of *ontological* inquiry. That said, obviously questions of epistemology aimed at recognizing a multivocal world within and without and ontological inquiries aimed at attuning to the polyphonic resonance of a more-than-human ecology are by no means mutually exclusive pursuits. Here, a hermeneutics of suspicion and doubt becomes entwined with a hermeneutics of insight and imagination to impel us towards "new" possibilities in a polysemous, polyphonous world. As Bringhurst has written: "The world is one, at the same time that it is plural, inherently plural, like the mind" (2006, p. 45).

২

Heidegger's thinking about the threat of machination, the way in which the world is increasingly enframed by the essence of technology, provides our final substrate. Due to an enigmatic writing style and vocabulary one might easily misinterpret his critique as straightforwardly anti-technology, but this is to miss both the substance of his insight and its pedagogical import. According to Heidegger, the genuine threat of technology does not lie, as one might assume, in the raw destructive force of feller bunchers or nuclear weaponry or "educational" mobile devices for infants, but in its monstrous capacity to *shape our relation with things*. For Heidegger technology is a "way of revealing" not a particular machine or device (1993, p. 318).

In his later writings, Heidegger describes machination as a logic of unconditional control and domination whereby nature is reduced to a "standing-reserve" and recognized only as an orderable "system of information" (p. 328). As Deluca maintains, this worldview of "explainability" is characterized by "calculation, giganticism, acceleration, and technicity wherein animals, plants and the earth become objects, mere resources, and humans, also, are reduced to the service of a ravenous progress" (2005, p. 76). While these observations may have been shocking and foreboding when they were originally delivered in the early 1950s, it is clear from this historical vantage point that machination is the order of the day.

> A recent *Business Week* headline announced, "Productivity Assured—or We'll Fix Them Free." It seems at first like the usual story about a warranty covering some new product. But not quite. A further glance reveals the article's subtitle: "Starting in 1994, L.A. high school grads will come with warranties".... Upon graduation, they will each "come with" a written warranty guaranteeing employers they possess the "basic skills needed to enter the work force." If they cannot perform these "basic skills" as advertised, they will be sent back for remediation at the District's expense. (Blackner, 1993, p. 1)

Utilizing the education system to convert children into production units (i.e., "standing reserves" or human resources) affirms some of Heidegger's worst fears about unfettered technological disclosure, and while his critical insights into our ontological condition are welcomed, his politics are not. Despite grave concerns, Heidegger construes the magnitude and reach of machination as essentially total and suggests, to a certain extent, that resistance is futile. I strongly share in Deluca's suggestion that we would do well to reject this defeatist mantra but maintain a Heidegger-inspired way of thinking to bring the ontological dimensions of technicity into question (2005, p. 76). In education, this entails courageous and sustained reflection upon our practices, artifacts, environments and organizational structures in order to determine if, and how, what we are doing is contributing to machination?

The neoliberal restructuring of education, for example, into an enterprise aimed at inculcating children into the austere realities of market capitalism provides an obvious instance of machination writ on the level of policy. As educational theorists David Hursh and Joseph Henderson (2011) have maintained, neoliberal policies have employed an all too familiar rhetoric of inevitability to limit public discourse, promote technical and market-based solutions in education, and decontextualize our knowledge and relationship with a place-based commons. The exploitative use-relation intrinsic to neoliberalism— as only the latest upgrade in a well-established lineage of instrumental rationality—is predicated upon the continued colonization, marginalization and silencing of the more-than-human. As we have seen, this deeply ingrained logic— what Heidegger called the "bewitchment of technicity" (1993, p. 86)—calls upon educators to maintain a position of disciplined hyperactive pessimism in order to critically assess the subtle and taken-for-granted.[5]

---

5   For more information on the undermining of environmental education by neoliberalism, see: "Sustainability and Education Policy Network," 2014. For place-based educational

For instance, while the neoliberal financialization of education presents a gross source of machinistic logic, what about something more commonplace like the use of nature imagery in the classroom? A Heideggerian approach to this question takes us deeper than conventional debates about whether technology is good, bad or neutral to its "essence" as a "way of revealing." In other words, the discourse around technology is taken beyond strategies for implementation or its relative pedagogical effectiveness into the more "metaphysical," but socio-politically pressing realms of ontological inquiry. Here, we are impelled down the path of asking questions like: what are the "ontological" costs of relying on high-definition photography and spectacular imagery as tools for inspiring care for the natural world? What sorts of revealing and kinds of relation does image-based technology (or any suite of technology for that matter) accord or foreclose with things? Or put into more succinct and critical terms, is it possible to challenge machination while using the techniques of machination (Deluca, 2005)?

ૐ

Poet Ted Hughes has veered down this path in his critique of education referring to the "morality of the camera" and describing the hollowing effects that technologically mediated objectivity can have on ethical agency. In his essay, "Myth and Education" (1988), he recounts an American magazine he happens upon one day depicting a tiger in the process of killing a woman. The tiger was "tame" and "belonged" to the woman and a professional photographer wanted to take some shots of them together, but something (perhaps the camera itself?) irritated the tiger and it began to attack and kill its "owner." As if that is not disturbing enough:

> Whatever his [the photographer's] thoughts were, he went on taking photographs of the whole procedure while the tiger killed the woman. The pictures were there in the magazine, but the story was told as if the photographer were absent, as if the camera had simply gone on doing what any camera would be expected to do, being a mere mechanical device for registering outward appearance. (1988, pp. 39-40)

Hughes is troubled by the way the camera in this scenario is not a neutral tool employed by a human agent but rather the means by which a human being is

---

alternatives to a neoliberal hegemony, see: Tuck & McKenzie, 2015; McKenzie, 2012; Gruenewald & Smith, 2008; Derby et al., 2015. For more on the negative impact of technology upon education, see: Bowers, 2008a, 2009 and Rose, 2013.

rendered an extension of mechanical registry. This is not to say that fending off an attacking tiger is an easy choice, but the sense that the situation calls for *something* more than objectively bearing witness and recording "data." This incident serves as an example for Hughes of the kind of humanity that results from an education centralized around objectivity and technicity. His educational ideal, on the other hand, reiterates the importance of the "inner world" and developing imaginative and affective faculties in order to know both inner and outer worlds (which are really one "all-inclusive system"). He claims this kind of knowing has been limited by technical objectivity, warning that the "exclusiveness of our objective eye, the very strength and brilliance of our objective intelligence, suddenly turns into stupidity—of the most rigid and suicidal kind" (pp. 38-39). We have become disconnected from our imaginative faculties because we have come to regard the inner experience and workings of the body as that of a "somewhat stupid vehicle" (p. 38). Hughes warns of an education that produces the kind of people who lack the capacity to see something *as* something (i.e., to see metaphorically, or as Wittgenstein would claim, to see-as) and who mechanically register information rather than participate within the affective, imaginative and reciprocal unfolding of things.

> They have to work on principles, on orders, or by precedent, and they will always be marked by extreme rigidity, because they are, after all, moving in the dark.... We all know such people, and we all recognize that they are dangerous since, if they have strong temperaments in other respects, they end up by destroying their environment and everybody near them. The terrible thing is that they are the planners, and ruthless slaves to the plan—which substitutes for the faculty they do not possess. And they have the will of desperation: Where others see alternative courses, they see only a gulf. (pp. 35-36)

The threat of machination in education—particularly in an age of ecological emergency—lies in strict adherence to the prescribed and fragmented curriculum of those who live in a myopic gulf of business as usual. In this sense, it makes little difference whether we allow cameras in the classroom or not, an education ordered along these lines is itself *technology* in a Heideggerian sense. A technology that manufactures distrust of imagination, myth, metaphor, our own bodies; a technology that alienates thinking from being and, despite our objective intelligence, turns into stupidity of the most rigid and ecocidal kind.

Chapter Five

ತ

To reiterate, from a Heideggerian perspective, it makes little sense to debate the educative value of, say, using digital cameras with zoom capabilities and high resolution versus mobile devices that allow for simpler images but internet access for a field trip to the park. Technology is not confined to particular devices but rather distributed throughout a system that reinforces a technicist relation. In this sense, the education system itself is technology; the motherboard of a machinistic worldview that, if we recall Blenkinsop, "carries with it the epistemology, ontology and axiology of the culture" (2012, p. 12). A Heideggerian approach is less concerned with the virtues or vices of digitalizing "instructional media" and more with how technology (read: education) lends itself to an increasingly univocal and anthropocentric encounter. As Heidegger warned, "In this way the illusion comes to prevail that everything man encounters exists only insofar as it is his construct. This illusion gives rise in turn to one final delusion: it seems as though man everywhere and always encounters only himself" (1993, p. 332).

The principal method of education as machination thus lies in silencing the more-than-human (Evernden, 1993). Its logic of severance and methods of objectivity are manufactured to foreclose relational possibilities and reduce knowing/being to calculation and yield such that humans are no longer able to even think outside the totalizing regime of technicity. In a world ordered along these lines loving affinity for nature is rendered romantic, education that centralizes emotional and imaginative engagement is rendered childish and fanciful, and the notion of meaningful communication with more-than-human beings? A *primitive* madness. As Heidegger carefully reiterates, the *real* threat of technology is that it expresses a fundamental lack of attentive consideration of a thing in its "many-sidedness." In other words, we become distracted and dissuaded of the interpretability and polyphonic structure of the world. Environmental education philosopher Michael Bonnett describes such encounters as a kind of insulation from wonder:

> A consequence of this totalitarianism over things (which of course includes ourselves, for we too are challenged forth and must assume the position and value allocated to us in the instrumental world picture) is that we are insulated from inspiration in the sense of the enrichment and refreshment afforded by encountering things afresh and in their inherent strangeness. Our view of the world becomes pre-formed, one track, closed off and thinking becomes "constipated." Thus, as the technological way of relating to the world gains ascendancy—which of course is central to its masterful nature—so we move along a road whose ultimate destination is nihilism in the sense of an empty

meaninglessness resulting from an inability to receive meaning from outside ourselves, our "self"-centered plans, calculations and definitions. It is under the influence of such thinking that the shining of a colour can be transformed into a wavelength, and the quiet, highly nuanced, presence of a wild flower in the grass can be transmuted into a crude (if highly precise) set of objective properties as it is slid into a scientific database. In each case the potential richness of the original experience is left behind as we move from participatory celebration to rational explanation, from receptiveness of emergent things to manipulating defined objects of thought. (2002, p. 235)

While a Heideggerian critique of technology compels us to critically reflect upon how education contributes to an instrumental world picture, an equally important and vital inquiry is how we might heal the severances of inveterate machination with pedagogical approaches that reveal the world beyond crude dominion and duality. But what could this possibly mean? Throwing all your cameras and computers into the big dumpster behind the school? Conducting classes outside in the wilderness where we might stay in contact with the potential richness of "original" experience? Neither of these strategies are without merit or precedent; Rudolf Steiner's Waldorf method famously prohibits, limits and delays the use of technological devices and often includes multi-day trips into wilderness (Clouder & Rawson, 2003; Blenkinsop, 2008), and there are place-based and forest school projects that are immersed outdoors in "natural environments" for much of the school year (Blenkinsop & Fettes, 2009; Fettes, 2013; Derby et al., 2013). That being said, an ecohermeneutic approach does not necessarily preclude the use of technological devices per se, rather it focuses on deliquescing the essence of technology as univocal encounter. As we have discussed in previous chapters, one of the fundamental means it imploys to achieve this is working on the level of metaphor in order to access the mythopoetic substratum of the dominant culture.

Once again Heidegger provides a potentially rich (albeit anthropocentric) substrate to cultivate ecological thinking by returning us to the significance of language, being and poetic encounter as an alternative to technicity: "Above all, enframing conceals that revealing which, in the sense of *poiesis*, lets what presences come forth into appearance" (1993, p. 332). As Heidegger tells us, only in the spontaneity and phenomenological magic of poetics can there be a *making* of the world; language establishes human being in the world and originally language was a poeticizing (Douglas, 2007). Heidegger's sense of the revealing capacity of *poiesis* here is related to the ancient Greek concept of *physis*. This notion is commonly translated into the static English noun "nature," but actually refers more to something like the "self-blossoming" emergence of things in time (something similar perhaps to Bonnett's "highly nuanced presence of a wild flower"). Heidegger's interest in the Greek presocratics was due to the significance they placed on the unfolding and emergent shape of poetic encounter. It serves to reason that if the presocratics were able to embody authentic modes of existence in which Being was revealed as a process of blossoming, then perhaps the way of the poet is still open to us?

An in-depth study of Heidegger's thinking on *poiesis* and its relationship to education is beyond the scope of this book (see Bonnett, 2002; Cooper, 2005; Douglas, 2007). As the first four chapters illustrated, ecohermeneutics shares in a kind of Heideggerian appreciation of poetic encounter, but *ecopoïesis*, it must be reiterated, emphasizes his anthropocentric limitations. Many of the ecologically-minded poets we have been thinking with—Zwicky, Bringhurst, and Lilburn amongst others (see Dickinson & Goulet, 2010)—have expressed similar suspicions of Heidegger's logocentric posturing and misled exaltation of poets. As Zwicky has warned, his valorization of *poiesis* does not, in the end, save us from the "brutal counter-finalities of technocratic approaches" (as cited in Elson, 2010, p. 88).

The history of modern poetry is in fact rife with poetic encounters that, on the surface, seem to exalt connection with the otherness of the natural world, but in actuality subtly reinforce the corralling of agential being into the anthropos. For example, in his journal, the American transcendentalist poet Ralph Waldo Emerson writes: "Language clothes Nature, as the air clothes the earth, taking the exact form and pressure of every object" (1965, p. 246). An ecohermeneutic orientation to language would reverse this such that language is understood as an emanation of a resonant topography that echoes the logics, forms and patterns of the ecologies from which it takes shape. In this sense, the origins of language do not lie in the poetic as Heidegger construes, but in the live, metaphoric resonance between human thinking and ecological form. Our use of language does not, as Heidegger claimed, endow us with superior ontological status, as Bringhurst has explained:

> Using language is as natural to humans as walking and running and picking things up. It is well to remember, however, that one species' nature is another species' artifice. Flying, not walking, is what comes naturally to bats. This does not make bats superior or inferior, nor closer to or farther away from the angels, nor does it mean that they possess immortal souls. It only means that they are bats. Martin Heidegger claimed that our abilities with language give members of the species *Homo sapiens* privileged metaphysical status, but this merely repeats at a grander level the error Heidegger made when he claimed that the two languages most inherently disposed to speak the truth

> were by coincidence two of the three or four languages he read, namely German and classical Greek. (2006, p. 128)

The revealing capacity of an ecopoetic approach—and its pedagogical significance—lies in recognizing that the more-than-human has its own voices and logics. It is for this reason that listening instead of dwelling (or rather, learning to dwell via listening) is the fundamental gesture of ecohermeneutic pedagogy.

chapter six

inoculating hermeneutics: Gadamer substrates

The Western legacy from Descartes has taught us to objectify the world from the position of pure subjectivity, a move which renders human experience of the world to a game between subjects and objects, and ensures the breakdown of genuine communication between persons and of relations between human and natural worlds. Hermeneutically, one speaks of the intersubjectivity of everything.... To see this, however, requires a particular kind of imaginal discipline, especially an ability to see connections which may not be superficially apparent. That very ability itself requires an openness to experience which goes beyond dependence on conventional categories of explanation, or on tradition received as a final word. Putting it in the language of postmodernism, the hermeneutic imagination requires an openness to the Other of experience, an openness to that which knocks from beyond the boundaries of what is known. To open the door means to have one's experience transformed into a new reality shared with new Others. (D. Smith, 1999, p. 46).

This chapter will consider a few of the key hermeneutic concepts of Hans-Georg Gadamer, student of Heidegger and perhaps the most renowned hermeneutic philosopher of the twentieth century. While Heidegger initiated the inquiry into being and interpretation, after the publication of *Being and Time* (1962), he ended his explicit engagement with hermeneutics and these aspects of his thinking were taken up by Gadamer, who spent thirty years composing his magnum opus *Truth and Method* (2013). In essence, Gadamer accepts Heidegger's ontological turn and acknowledges interpretation—our prior hermeneutical situatedness or pre-understanding—as a primordial condition of human experience. He also shares in the notion that method can never achieve universal applicability because it bears the same character and quality as that which it seeks to grasp (i.e., "methodological thinking" can never be made independent from the historical conditioning of thinking in general). Gadamer develops this hermeneutics of "historically effected consciousness" (p. 350) by claiming that the appropriate method for interpreting any phenomenon can only be disclosed by the phenomenon itself through a kind of dialogical engagement between question and phenomenon (D. Smith, 1999). His project never intended to provide a new technique for textual exegesis or a comprehensive methodology for the human sciences, but remained philosophic in nature: "not what we do or what we ought to do, but what happens to us over and above our wanting and doing" (2013, p. xxvi; also see Jardine, 2006).

Two Heideggerian concepts greatly enriched by Gadamer are of central importance to the germination of an ecohermeneutic imagination. The first is the historicity of understanding, the historico-temporal quality of experience; and the second is the linguisticality of understanding, the linguistic mediation of knowing. We touched on a Heideggerian understanding of historicity in the previous chapter and offered a brief ecohermeneutic reading of some related concepts (i.e., background, pre-understanding and co-constitutionality). Similarly, in this chapter, Gadamerian substrates will be inoculated in order to remediate the landscape for the possibility of sharing a new educational reality that recognizes the significance of more-than-human alterity. As D. Smith has maintained, the principal texts of the hermeneutic tradition do not restrict us to dogmatic prescriptions, but open the imagination to creative, interdisciplinary and expedient possibilities: "...the hermeneutic imagination is not limited in its conceptual resources to the texts of the hermeneutic tradition itself but is liberated by them to bring to bear any conceptualities that can assist in deepening our understanding of what it is we are investigating" (1999, p. 41). So while Gadamer remains, to a certain extent, embedded in some of the logocentric and anthropocentric premises of his time, an ecohermeneutic imagination aims to recycle what remains vibrant in his dialogical approach and connect it with the conceptualities of contemporary ecocritical theory. In fact, this act of recycling and keeping traditions relevant to our living is precisely part of what Gadamer posits as central to hermeneutics itself.

ৡ

Gadamer develops the Heideggerian notion of a historical fore-structure of understanding by proposing that *prejudice* (i.e., "pre-judgment") is a necessary requirement of knowing and that we only make sense of the world from within a particular cultural-historical "horizon." Understanding is thus only possible to the degree that one is able to enter into conversation and bring about a "fusion" of different horizons (2013, p. 350). This is not to claim that we are in any way beholden to or entrenched in a given tradition but, as D. Smith claims, Gadamerian hermeneutics validates "a new appreciation of tradition as the received life-stream out of which it is possible to say or do anything at all" (1999, p. 33). Situating understanding within a localized horizon or form of life is an intentional move, in part, to counter the objectivist thrust of the natural sciences and claims that knowledge can be freed from human interest and historical flux. While these humanist claims offer an effective counterpoise to the privileging of universalist and essentialist positions, they also tend to delineate a human-centric horizon of meaning beyond which there is the aesthetic address of nature "for us," but otherwise a perspective-less and non-agential taciturnity. The world remains silenced.

Environmental philosopher Mick Smith has explored the "expressivist hermeneutics" of Gadamer (and Walter Benjamin), arguing that both philosophers understood language as an "expression of being" and might thus be used to broaden the "anthropic conception of language and address the possibility of interpreting non-human expressions in determinate ways" (2001b, p. 60). Before we recycle Gadamer to these ends, however, it is important to underline the degree to which Gadamer fell in line with the humanist hegemony of privileging culture over nature. As the following passage illustrates, there is both a troubling anthropic hubris in Gadamer's thinking and great promise as a means of understanding how *language* might come to include the gestural significance and address of more-than-human meaning.

> Precisely because in nature we find no *ends in themselves* and yet find beauty—i.e., a suitedness to the end of our pleasure, nature gives us a "hint" that we are in fact the ultimate end, the final goal of creation. The dissolution of the ancient cosmological thought that assigned man his place in the total structure of being and assigned each entity its goal of perfection gives the world, which ceases to be beautiful as a structure of absolute ends, the new *beauty* of being purposive for us. It becomes "nature," whose innocence consists in the fact that it knows nothing of man or his social vices. Nevertheless, it has something to say to us. As beautiful, nature finds a *language* that brings to *us* an intelligible idea of what mankind is to be. (2013, p. 47)

Despite the heavy-handed humanism, one can appreciate the attempt to move beyond "nature" as a knowable operation of immutable laws and absolute ends towards a dialogical, emergent and aesthetically compelling relation in which we participate and learn. Gadamer was interested in merging the notion of historicity with the German humanist tradition of *Bildung*—the concept of *self-formation, education, or cultivation*; or as Johann Herder defined it, "rising up to humanity through culture" (as cited in Gadamer, 2013, p. 9). He differed from his classicist counterparts, however, in that rising into the "cult of Bildung" was not like rising towards the social conventions of high culture or coming into the universal essence of the spirit; rather, he points to the way the continuous process of Bildung and the Greek concept of nature as *physis* are similar: "like nature, Bildung has no goals outside itself" (pp. 10-11). His thinking on historicity and his critique of absolutism directly challenged the excessive vanity of Enlightenment idolization of culture in the sense that one could be "lifted up" above the rawness of nature and progress towards perfect and complete humanity. For Gadamer, such sentiments were indicative of "the arrogant confidence of modernity at its beginnings" (1998, p. 1).

The problem with Gadamer's conception of Bildung, however, is that he uncritically accepts nature/culture dualism and, for the most part, construes "becoming cultured" as distancing oneself from nature. As M. Smith has maintained, "this distancing is facilitated by our particular ability to share in human language, in the communality of the word" (2001b, p. 72). Despite the non-teleological and *physis*-like emergence of learning to be human in Gadamerian thought and the aesthetic *language* of the natural world, nature consistently figures in his thinking as "dumb contrast" to the volubility of culture. In keeping with his suspicion about absolute and "natural" ends, he remains concerned about indeterminate interpretations of nature according to mood (i.e., subjectivism, Romanticism) and Kantian positions that claim nature is capable of delivering moral monologues (i.e., the naturalization of social formations) (p. 61). Rather, Gadamer subscribes to humanist notions of Bildung and considers culture, language and ethics coeval with the educative development of humanity away from animalistic and deep-rooted instincts of aggression. So while this rising towards humanity is less deterministic and arrogant than previous notions of enculturation, culture remains defined in opposition to nature and is that which "stops men from assaulting one another, and from being worse than any animal" (Gadamer, 1998, p. 10).

An ecohermeneutic understanding seeks to further entangle the coevolving interdependence of Bildung and *physis* in order to bring the process of becoming educated into resonance with the unfolding dialectic of agential and material interrelatedness. This pedagogy, as we have seen, imploys historical analysis, metaphor, contemplative practice and immersive experience to draw

Chapter Six

students towards recognizing more-than-human alterity. In an ecohermeneutic formulation of Bildung, we rise, or rather return (bending low in humility towards the earth) to our "humanity" via the cultivation of a resonant relation with the ecology of what-is; and to the extent that we sever this relation, silence the other, and poison the generative humus of our interbeing—we forsake the possibility of being "human" (as opposed to a human-like standing reserve). Ecohermeneutic inoculation thus works to disclose our historically derived prejudice regarding more-than-human alterity, as this received life-stream forms both the substrate of our present understanding and the means to mushroom beyond.

ॐ

Many educational theorists, particularly ecologically-minded educators, have been drawn to Gadamerian hermeneutics (Jardine, 1998, 2006; Sammel, 2003; Grun, 2005; Fettes, 2013). For these educationists, Gadamer offers the possibility of coming to understand the immense complexity of the ecological crisis in the context of its historical emergence and gain a sense of how we might veer towards more ecojust ways of learning and being. Nevertheless, Cartesian cultural tenets are deep-seated and although important revisions and refinements have been made in education, we tend to remain at the deepest levels of our thought process, Cartesian thinkers (Bowers, 1993). As Brazilian educationalist Mauro Grun has maintained, one of the elements that prevents deeper understanding of ecological interrelatedness is the autonomy of a detached subject as an educational ideal:

> In Cartesian epistemology the observer sees nature as if looking at a photograph. There is an "I" who thinks, and the thing that is thought of; this thing is the world turned object. The autonomous subject is someone outside of nature. This process of separation results in the objectification of nature. The autonomy of the thinking subject, free of cultural values and through its independence from the environment, is constituted as the very basis of education, rather than being seen as a possible deficiency. The Cartesian cogito is thus the basis of education. (2005, p. 158)

This "process" of learning to sever oneself from the world via "autonomous thinking" is unmistakably reminiscent of Heidegger's critique of technological enframing. As Heidegger implied, the crux of the problem here does not lie with the use of image-based devices, but with the education system as a technology that contributes to machination and reduces relational capacity to something objectively photographic in essence (also see Evernden, 1993). The ontological dimension is important to underline here lest we continue incorporating "environmental issues" such as climate change, energy alternatives or deforestation into the curriculum without acknowledging the ways in which these topics become immediately "trapped within the fine mesh of Cartesian discourses" (Grun, 2005, p. 158). In other words, if the relational essence remains entrenched in instrumental rationality and the natural world continues to be backgrounded, objectified and colonized, it makes little difference how much environmental content is tacked onto the curriculum. The form belies the content. If, however, the presuppositions informing subject/object and culture/nature duality are so deeply ingrained—how are we to access the substratum of our present form of life?

As discussed in previous chapters, an ecohermeneutic response is to focus more intentionally on the linguistic and mythopoetic dimensions of ecologically destructive patterns of thought as a means of working on the level of cultural transformation. This entails a pedagogy committed to ecocritical discourse analysis in order to foreground the historical emergence of, for example, the autonomous subject as an educational ideal, and begin deliquescing rigid and self-evident certainties within the present horizon. It also means walking the difficult path of ontological inquiry towards more liminal and underground free spaces where we are able to voice questions like: What would it mean to view the "I" as a possible deficiency in education? How might we co-create educational encounters that problematize "autonomous thinking" by encouraging "ecological thinking" *with* place? How do we move from education as a technology geared towards resourcism and use-relations towards education as an ecopoetic encounter characterized by "attentiveness, precision, and a tenderness towards existence" (Fisher-Wirth & Street, 2013, p. xxvii)?

Ecocritical analysis could, broadly speaking, be characterized as hermeneutic illumination of our historically effected *ecological* consciousness in a Gadamerian sense. Although ecocritical theory in pedagogy has been much expanded in recent decades by theorists in fields such as ecojustice education (Bowers, 1993; Martusewicz et al., 2011), ecopedagogy (Kahn, 2010; Lewis & Kahn, 2010; Pierce, 2013), ecophilosophy (Jardine, 1998; Bonnett, 2004), place-based pedagogy (Gruenewald & Smith, 2008; McKenzie, Hart, Bai & Jickling, 2009), ecofeminism (Russell & Bell, 1996; Fawcett, 2000) and Indigenous pedagogies of decolonization (Chambers, 1999; Donald, 2009; Battiste, 2013; Tuck & McKenzie, 2015)—not to mention the proliferation of ecocritical theory in fields beyond education (Cronon, 1995; Bennett, 2010; Morton, 2010; Goodbody &

Rigby, 2011, to name but a few). So while Gadamer's thinking on historicity was, in a sense, an antecedent and indispensable substrate in the development of ecological consciousness as a kind of post-Cartesian sensibility, any pedagogy concerned with the historicity of ecological understanding would be greatly enriched by sustained connection and consideration of more contemporary ecocritical theory. Finding the language to enable critical understanding of the complexity of the ecological crisis is, after all, one of the most significant challenges facing educators, and ecocritical pedagogies offer much by focusing on historical emergence and the metaphoric roots of the linguistic dimension.

There is a way, however, in which even these approaches can manifest a kind of "experiential logocentrism" if they are not thoughtfully coupled with meaningful and immersive encounters with the more-than-human world (or to put it haphazardly, if they do not also "get into contact with wild(er)ness"). So while ecocritical analysis is a crucial, again we must return to the importance of making space for encountering more-than-human otherness on its own terms (Derby et al., 2015). As M. Smith has written, "somewhere along the line other aspects of nature must enter human discourse," and that it is only our "modern form of life that stops us recognizing that nature too can impart something of itself just as immediately and just as magically as the human word" (2001, p. 72).

This is a pressing concern for ecohermeneutic educators as the most immediate and obvious limitation to ecological understanding in the biology and history classroom—or even the woodworking shop—is not a lack of nuanced ecocritical discourse, but the absence-like marginalization of more-than-human presence such that there is no occasion for even the possibility of "ecopoetic encounter." Ecohermeneutic educators not only need to get beyond our historical horizon, they need to get beyond the walls of the conventional classroom in order to meaningfully engage the body and imagination (Fettes, 2011, 2013). But what makes these encounters meaningful? How do we move from walks in the park towards a pedagogy that co-teaches with place? In order to explore this pedagogical move, we must consider the relationship between a Gadamerian sense of *language* and more-than-human meaning.

ৡ

In his critique of the Cartesian basis of education, Grun (2005) claims there is much it does not allow "by dint of its projection of itself as the only possible mode of comprehending reality," and that we must address its conceptual inadequacies by bringing to the foreground all the "areas of silence" it conceals

(p. 162). These areas of silence include the ways in which the education system has traditionally remained silent (until at least the 1980s) on the ecological destruction wrought by industrial societies (Bowers & Flinders, 1990), but also the way place itself is silenced via modernist-scientific thinking tempered by emancipation from locality as an ideal. Within this form of life, place has "lost its authenticity and its meaning" as vernacular commons have been enclosed by commercial interests (Bowers, 1993) and as we have subsequently lost the ability to recognize the particularities and significance of place (Grun, 2005, p. 163). The modern mind has thus come to view human social practice as the sole source of meaning and acknowledges the expressive capacity of place only to the extent that it conforms to measure and instrumental yield. Although the postmodern turn in recent decades has challenged many of the hallmarks of Cartesianism—mind/body duality, the autonomous subject, and logocentrism, to name a few—these critiques have yet to extend beyond the horizon of human in a substantive way in order to foreground the communicative meaning of place and more-than-human beings. As Bringhurst explains:

> The postmodernist view is (1) that the place to look for meanings is in relations involving human beings and (2) that these relations may be altogether different for different human beings. That opinion is now very widely held—in amusement parks and universities, in the city and on the reserve. I take a different view myself. It seems to me that things have meaning before they are ever seen or touched by human beings, and that humans can participate, as trees can, in the meaning-making process. I think that humans can put meanings into things in such a way that they will stay where they are put, and other humans can come by, even centuries later, and draw those meanings out. Some meanings—if that is the right word for them—are highly individual; some are peculiar to certain communities and cultures; but there is a rich fund of meanings that is shared by the whole species, and a fund of meanings richer yet that is the common property not of the species but of the planet. (2006, p. 213)

Language expressed as words remains the paradigmatic medium of human thought and communication and as such we have tended to deny mental being to everything lacking "language" (M. Smith, 2001b).

Once again, these sentiments seem reminiscent of the crux of Heidegger's question concerning technology; namely that the threat of enframing lies in its concealment of alternative modes of revealing which, in the sense of *poiesis*, "lets what presences come forth into appearance" (1993, p. 332). But what does this mean? How might we come to discern the presence of things or places as *physis*-like processes of unfolding instead of objects that *do* something for us? And even if we could, what does *presence* communicate? In the spirit of reading

Heidegger's "after-philosophy" (Deluca, 2005), we want to avoid conflating respect for things in their unfolding with respect for their metaphysical essence (i.e., being-in-itself) or as absolute ends in themselves. As Grun notes, Gadamer navigates this metaphysical hazard by arriving at a model of understanding that is dialogical or dialectic, "Gadamer thus argues that to query the nature of things is inappropriate, and proposes that it should be replaced by querying the language of things" (2005, p. 164). In regarding language as a direct expression of being as such (as opposed to an expression of some interior psychological state of mind), Gadamer proposes an ontology of language and meaning that challenges Cartesian dualism between an *immaterial language of thought* and the *thoughtless materiality of the world* (M. Smith, 2001b, p. 65).

> Our inquiry has been guided by the basic idea that language is a medium where I and world meet or, rather, manifest their original belonging together. We have also shown that this speculative medium that language is represents a finite process in contrast to the infinite dialectical mediation of concepts. In all the cases we analyzed—in the language of conversation, of poetry, and also of interpretation—the speculative structure of language emerged, not as the reflection of something given but as the coming into language of a totality of meaning.... This activity of the thing itself is the real speculative moment that takes hold of the speaker. We have sought the subjective reflection of it in speech. We can now see that this activity of the thing itself, the coming into language of meaning, points to a universal ontological structure, namely to the basic nature of everything towards which understanding can be directed. *Being that can be understood is language*. The hermeneutical phenomenon here projects its own universality back onto the ontological constitution of what is understood, determining in it a universal sense as *language* and determining its own relation to beings as interpretation. Thus we speak not only of a language of art but also a language of nature—in short, of any language that things have. (2013, p. 490).

Despite some anthropocentric tendencies elsewhere, in this passage, Gadamer clearly considers coming into language as a participatory reciprocity between self and world, a dialectic such that human no longer stands apart from nature. Thus inoculated, the category of *language* deliquesces from being a hallmark of human exceptionalism and the definitive boundary between nature/culture and reemerges as the medium where we manifest our original and ecological belonging together. Read ecohermeneutically, being that can be understood—including the significance of gesture and the "extra-linguistic" dimensions of our dialectic with the more-than-human world—is *language*. As M. Smith has illustrated, this understanding of language shares much with

Walter Benjamin's (1998) attempt to get beyond Cartesian dualism by radically redefining what comprises language.

> The existence of language, however, is not only coextensive with all the areas of human mental expression in which language is always in one sense or another inherent, but with absolutely everything. There is no event or thing in either animate or inanimate nature that does not in some way partake of language, for it is in the nature of all to communicate their mental meanings. (p. 107)

Once *language* is no longer an exclusive human feature and is redefined as a material capacity for expression, there is no reason such communicative ability should be limited only to human interlocutors. This does not, it must be noted, completely remove the humanist bias in Gadamerian hermeneutics; "being that can be understood" does not necessarily bestow subjectivity or perspective to the more-than-human other. As M. Smith has warned, "Nature's linguistic being is not that which nature is capable of expressing but is confined to that which actually makes an impression on humanity in a form that we can put into words" (2001b, p. 68). Be that as it may, Gadamer's emphasis on the indeterminate unfolding of "linguistic traditions"—the historically effected and liquid horizon that constitutes our form of life—as the ultimate source of meaningful engagement offers a pedagogically significant means of moving beyond the anthropic prejudice that characterized his time. This is, in essence, the critical ecohermeneutic interest in pedagogy as a means of cultural transformation; the move from one generation recognizing the linguistic address of nature to the next listening with the more-than-human other as an ontologically robust co-teacher. Put differently, an ecohermeneutic mind understands *language* in a Gadamerian sense as *resonance*.

A final comment on beauty. Some of the troubling Romantic and human-centered comments Gadamer has made with respect to the mindless innocence of nature or its capacity for language in the beautiful might also be recycled in light of the dialogical and participatory ontology at the core of his hermeneutics. For Gadamer, the address of the beautiful as a concept and as a common experience lent itself most readily to the hermeneutic notion of recognizing meaning in the activity of the thing itself (his inquiry also draws on the language of conversation, poetry and translation to similar ends). Jumping off the skygazing pyramid of human exceptionalism into the messy web of ecological entanglement was, in a sense, too far a leap beyond the horizon. The experience of being moved by the beauty of nature or a compelling work of art, however, was well within the experiential lexicon of his time and culture. Gadamer draws on the aesthetic experience as a means of understanding the address of the other, the experience of being elicited by something over and above our wanting and doing. Language as it is conventionally understood is only subjective reflection upon "the real speculative moment" that takes hold of the speaker. Again, Gadamerian hermeneutics seems to converge here with the attentive discipline at the heart of an ecopoetic approach to pedagogy. Learning about environmental issues and developing an ecocritical understanding are both constitutive elements, but at a certain point we must also develop the discipline to *recognize* more-than-human alterity and, as Grun (2005) has maintained, engage with nature on its own terms.

> In art the experience is always one of being confronted by someone or something; of being seduced or challenged by the simple fact of otherness. Consequently nature itself will not be heard until we engage with it on its own terms. That is not to say that nature loses its dignity, but rather to argue that nature, like the work of art, becomes itself in the act of self-representation. This understanding is only possible when we retain respect for the thing, for its otherness. (p. 163).

Gadamer has written "the best definition for hermeneutics is: to let what is alienated by the character of the written word or by the character of being distantiated by cultural or historical distances speak again. This is hermeneutics: to let what seems to be far and alienated speak again" (as cited in Gallagher, 1992, p. 4). The more-than-human world has been traditionally construed as the antithesis of culture, even within the hermeneutic tradition, our experience of it has been alienated by the character of the written word. This is the task of an ecohermeneutic approach to education, to make space for the more-than-human to speak again and develop the mindfulness to listen.

> Mindfulness of our rootedness in Earthly experiences is a breakthrough to the belonging-together of things that goes on without us, without our doing. It is a realization of the deep Earthly collectivity of things that is not of our own making, wanting, or doing. In one formulation, hermeneutics seems to verge near this: the hermeneutic project is concerned with, "not what we do or what we ought to do, but what happens to us over and above our wanting and doing" (Gadamer, 2004). But this hermeneutic project still remains a matter of Eurocentric enculturation, lacking the scent and the fragrance of and the fleshy intersections of an Earth that "happens" (even if it *doesn't* happen "to us") and to which we are indebted in silent ways that speak neither Greek nor German.

In mindfulness of this silent collectivity of the Earth, there is an archaic debt at work, the debt of breath and blood and sun and soil and sky, and all those hopelessly naïve things the forgetting of which threatens to suddenly and violently trivialize our urbane theorizing with unspeakable ecological events that we, in all our earnestness, cannot outrun or sidestep. (Jardine, 1998, p. 87) chapter seven

hermeneutics deep in the clearcut

> of the thousands of things
> we always forget
> millions of larger-than-human things
> accomplish the three Rs
>   *from*   *to*   and   *of*
> even the smallest of streams
>   (Denholm, 2014, p. 16)

Let's take a soil sample of the educational landscape. What are some of the cultural values and conventions the Canadian education system cultivates in future generations? Not specific prescribed learning outcomes or the "core competencies" evident in all areas of learning, but a sample of the *topos* from which our educational experiences emerge. Notwithstanding the potential fecundity of the intellectually rich traditions, disciplines and cultural artifacts that comprise the curriculum[1] or the commitment of particular teachers to impart and model reflexive ways of thinking and an ethics of care—the substratum of education remains constituted by competition, abstraction, compliance, fatalism and

---

1   This is not to imply that the curriculum is culturally neutral or that its content and delivery are not, at times, overtly and innately racist, sexist, classist, anthropocentric, etc. The problem with curriculum has less to do with Shakespeare, Pythagorean theorem and the scientific method as inherently problematic materials for learning, and more to do with the way they are afforded epistemic privilege, divorced from place-based resonance and critical historical analysis, and delivered in an environment comprised of deep-seated and ecologically destructive cultural values that remain beyond question.

dominion. Environmental educators Sean Blenkinsop and Chris Beeman add to the sample:

> ...mobility without penalty; perceived isolation or independence from the ecological processes that actually keep us alive; a historically unprecedented use of non-renewables to satisfy wants more than needs; generally fragmented human relations reduced to short-term interactions, normally for instrumental purposes; competitiveness; the culture of the individual; the culture of the human; and the hubristic conception of linear human progression to a position of superiority over what has gone before in human and ecosystem history. (2008, p. 16)

All education, as environmental theorist David Orr (2005) reminds us, is environmental education by virtue of what is included or excluded in the learning experience. This does not mean, however, that incorporating "sustainability course content" or "place-based experiences" into the curriculum necessarily alters the topos of learning. Something else is called for, something that reaches deep into the groundwork of our understanding and cultivates "curriculum languages and genres that name the sociopolitical, geophysical and imaginative landscape in which Canadians live now," by seeking "new interpretive tools for understanding" (Chambers, 1999, p. 137). In an age of ecological emergency, educators stand exigently at the paradoxical moment of the re-birth of humanity, or—if we do nothing to remediate the contaminated soils of our historically effected consciousness—the *degenerativity* of humanity, the desecration of our shared flesh and humus. As Jardine has maintained, something is called for in these times that goes beyond "one more damn thing," beyond one more theory or curricular addendum to be "dumped on the pile with others in our onrush to ecological self-consumption" (1998, p. 12).

Critical ecohermeneutics, to reiterate, is a philosophic mycorestoration strategy aimed at inoculating the substrates of modern thought in order to revitalize the degraded substratum of being. While a remedial disposition lies at the heart of ecohermeneutic work, it eschews becoming one more damn thing on the pile in its commitment to ecocritical reflexivity and praxis in education as a means of radical cultural transformation. This is the mycelial-like and deliquescent activity of ecohermeneutics as a pedagogical intervention in alliance and affinity with oppressed communities and the subaltern, including more-than-human communities (Blenkinsop & Beeman, 2010). Education as mycological membrane; a keystone activity in the generation of ever-thickening layers of ecological understanding that make way for future generations and forms of life to flourish.

> The activities of mycelium help heal and steer ecosystems on their evolutionary path, cycling nutrients through the food chain. As land masses and mountain ranges form, successive generations of plants and animals are born, live and die. Fungi are keystone species that create ever-thickening layers of soil, which allow future plants and animal generations to flourish. Without fungi, all ecosystems would fail.
>
> Mushroom spawn lets us recycle garden waste, wood, and yard debris, thereby creating mycological membranes that heal habitats suffering from poor nutrition, stress and toxic waste. In this sense, mushrooms emerge as environmental guardians in a time critical to our mutual evolutionary survival. (Stamets, 2005, p. 1)

Education, understood ecohermeneutically, thus emerges fungi-like from the clearcut slash of conventional learning, feeding on and recycling the debris of fragmented thinking, healing the landscape from epistemicides, and provoking a mycelial imagination informed by lyric realism, eco-constitutionality, and an interpretive disposition that makes space for a multispecies and panelemental approach to learning. Without fungi, all ecocultural systems fail.

In order to explore the need for ecohermeneutic understanding in education, we turn our attention to inoculating "environmental education" itself by underlining the way ontological inquiries and more-than-human alterity tend to be marginalized, even in "critical" approaches. In other words, while ecological understanding and literacy are often touted as the panacean counter measure to blindspots in the conventional system, we must revisit whether "environmental education," in its prevailing form, is what is called for? Does environmental education, for example, dig deep enough to disrupt the technicist ontology or the autonomous subject that underlies modern education? Or is the field at threat of being appropriated by an encroaching neoliberal agenda that employs sustainability education to greenwash industrialist excesses whilst reaffirming the core values and presuppositions of the dominant culture (Derby et al., 2015)?[2]

Despite decades of "environmental consciousness" and educational initiatives we are hard pressed to point to any transformative shifts in dominant cultural behavior or ethos towards our deep implicatedness in the natural world (Joldersma, 2009). Blenkinsop and Fettes (2009), for example, describe the "limited gains" made by environmental education in recent decades:

> Public education systems, across the industrialized world, tend to be isolated from local processes of knowledge building, planning, and decision-making for sustainability.

---

[2] For more on the relationship between neoliberal policies and environmental education see the Sustainability and Education Policy Network (SEPN) hosted at the University of Saskatchewan: http://sepn.ca.

> In addition, although efforts have been made over the last three decades to include environmental education in school programs, their overall impact has been limited. Environmental education programs are rarely integrated with the mainstream curriculum, are typically of short duration, often lack theoretical or methodological sophistication, and show little compelling evidence of having long-term effects on most students' thinking about or engagement with diverse others including the natural world. (p. 1)

Judson (2010) echoes these sentiments:

> The development of what some call *ecological understanding* is often cited as the aim of Ecological Education. To understand ecologically is to make sense of the human world as part of, not apart from, nature; it is to understand humankind's "implicatedness in life" (Orr, 2005, p. 105). The problem, however, is that Ecological Education is ill-equipped to achieve this aim. (p. 1)

> On one level, the field as a whole is limited. Its marginal status in schools makes its aim to change students' perceptions of the world at best optimistic and at worst delusional. But simply moving the practice of Ecological Education in its prevailing form from the margins to the center of schools is not going to make it effective. There are deeper problems with Ecological Education practice when one considers its aims and how it attempts to achieve these. (p. 25)

If we mark the 1962 publication of Rachel Carson's *Silent Spring* as the initial moment of a gradual mainstreaming of environmental consciousness in North America (amongst non-Indigenous peoples), we could say that environmental education has been active for just over fifty years. Despite the recent swell of public interest in issues such as climate change and biodiversity and a UN decade devoted to Education for Sustainable Development, business remains, by and large, as usual (Huckle & Wals, 2015).

> Populations are still increasing, degradation of the planet is expanding, resource consumption is growing exponentially, and, for the most part, those who are responsible, the privileged of the west and north, continue to fiddle, like modern day Neros, while the globe burns. Ironically, they are also the most likely to have been exposed to environmental education. (Blenkinsop, 2012)

Orr (1991) has similarly observed that the ecological crisis is not necessarily the work of "ignorant people," rather that of the "well-educated" populations of developed nations (also see Serres, 2010). By way of analogy, Orr reminds us that the perpetrators of the Jewish Holocaust were the direct heirs of Kant and Goethe, and that the Germans were widely regarded as some of the best-educated people on earth before and during the rise of National Socialism. This begs the question: what characterized their education? He cites Elie Wiesel in response, "It emphasized theories instead of values, concepts rather than human beings, abstraction rather than consciousness, answers instead of questions, ideology and efficiency rather than conscience" (as cited in Orr, 1991, p. 52). While her response is fundamentally "humanistic," the essence—a critique of the dehumanizing logic of machination at the core of education—is an accurate description of the present and emerging system in Canada and across the industrialized world. Orr traces the foundations of these educational ideals back to the usual suspects of Enlightenment thought: Francis Bacon, Galileo Galilei and Rene Descartes.

Despite maligning a "Cartesian" ontology myself in previous chapters, I question the ease with which we sometimes place blame so squarely upon the heads of these tragically grand thinkers? Developing critical consciousness and tracing some of our ontological presuppositions back to their historical proponents is one thing, transferring blame for the ecologically destructive apparatus and habits of our everyday lives onto a patently monstrous historical icon is quite another. As Orr has implied, there is a disconcerting analogy to be made between the everyday responsibility for the rise of the Third Reich and our own ecological bootprints. The individualist bias in the way we learn history often leaves one with the sense that Hitler was a manipulative brainwasher who indoctrinated a credulous and susceptible German population into carrying out the Holocaust like automated cogs in a fated machine. While elements of this view are accurate to a certain extent, it is important, as Orr maintains, to keep in mind that the Third Reich was rationalized, justified and executed by a well-educated populace of workaday, rational citizens. Or as Jürgen Habermas has hauntingly described it: "The monstrous occurred without interrupting the smooth breathing of everyday life" (1990, p. 208).

The analogy lends itself to a troubling but important set of questions for educators in a time of ecological crisis. Are we, or rather how are we, rationalizing and justifying the extermination of human and more-than-human life on a Holocaust-like scale of global extinction? To what extent does the education system contribute to reproducing the technicist logic required for justifying ecocidal resource extraction or the absurd notion that we can have planetary mobility without penalty? To what extent does becoming "well-educated" entail losing the ability to hear the "vocal cords of the world" (Evernden, 1993)? Or as Orr has put it plainly, in a time of ecological emergency: what is education for?

Orr is not alone in drawing connections between the technicist domination politics and educational policies of the Third Reich and the logic of machination underlying industrial and neoliberal capitalism. Ecophilosopher Derrick Jensen (2002) has warned of the invisibility and encroaching familiarity with which twenty-first century holocausts might become established.

> Each holocaust is unique. The destruction of the European Jewry did not look like the destruction of the American Indians. It could not because the technologies involved were not the same, the targets were not the same, and the perpetrators were not the same.... And, just as similarly, the holocausts of the twenty-first century will not, and do not already look like the great holocausts of the twentieth...
>
> What will the great holocausts of the twenty-first century look like? It depends on where you stand. Look around.
>
> The holocaust will look like numbers on ledgers. It will look like technical problems to be solved, whether those problems are increasing your access to necessary resources, dealing with global warming, calming unrest on the streets, or figuring out what to do about too many unproductive people on land that could be put to better use.... The holocaust will feel like economics. It will feel like progress. It will feel like technological innovation. It will feel like civilization. It will feel like the way things are. (pp. 592–594)
>
> Maybe it feels like salmon battering themselves against dams, monkeys locked in steel cages, polar bears starving on a dwindling ice cap, hogs confined in crates so small they cannot stand, trees falling to the chainsaw, rivers poisoned, whales deafened by sonic blasts from Navy experiments. Maybe it feels like the crack of tibia under the unforgiving jaws of a leghold trap. (p. 596)

Maybe it feels like doom and gloom reality checks, bringing children up to speed on glacial recession rates and ozone depletion, punishing them by picking up litter, dissecting little animals with analytical indifference? Maybe it feels rational and realistic like incorporating the business-inspired objectives of "sustainable development" because growth is inevitable? Maybe it feels like solution-based thinking and staying positive despite the odds, installing recycling bins and energy-saving lightbulbs in the classroom? What is called for from this deep in the clearcut?

I want to believe that environmental education offers a way beneath the surface; that sustainability education and eco-friendly lifestyle choices might deliver on the promise of a new kind of ecological understanding. But there is little historical evidence and if environmental education is aimed at *ecologizing* future generations there is a sense that the strategy thus far does not correspond to the profound transformation required by the crisis. French philosopher Bruno Latour voiced a similar concern at the 2009 Henry Myers lecture for the Royal Institute of Anthropology:

What is not clear is what *ecologizing* will mean exactly. The range of attitudes, prescriptions, warnings, restrictions, summons, sermons and threats, that go with ecology seems to be strangely out of sync with the magnitude of the changes expected from all of us.... When the first tremors of the Apocalypse are heard, it would seem that preparations for the end should require something more than simply using a different kind of lightbulb... (p. 462)

Something more is called for, something thought provoking but also heartfelt, something curative but also uncompromising and fierce when it needs to be, something meaningful, something *critical*. But what does critical mean?

ৡ

The term *critical environmental education* has gained some prominence in academic circles in recent years.[3] Science and sustainability educator Ali Sammel defines the term as representative of "pedagogies that strive to expose the taken for granted assumptions underpinning the content and process of teaching environmental issues while seeking action around injustices occurring as a result of our dominant cultural narrative" (2003, p. 157). Critical ecohermeneutics might be described in similar terms in that it shares a kinship with ecocritical pedagogies seeking to move beyond the existing hegemonic structures that reproduce social and ecological injustice. There is little in the literature, however, regarding the philosophy of language or the ontological leanings that inform critical environmental education. While Sammel (2003) has employed Gadamerian hermeneutics as a research methodology to interpret how a group of teachers make sense of implementing ecocritical pedagogy, there is no mention, for example, of using Gadamer to expand the hermeneutic imagination beyond the horizon of human.

The *critical* modifier on ecohermeneutics is not added for the purposes of academic signage, allegiance or adornment. One is left with the sense these days that the term "critical" serves more as a rhetorical strategy for mobilizing a tradition in support of an argument, instead of indicating/enacting a seditious challenge to dominant narratives and a commitment to a living, fire-breathing praxis. While being critical of the ecological injustices perpetuated by industrial capitalism is obviously an important aspect of ecocritical inquiry, I maintain that critical environmental education ought to dig deeper to trouble and remediate the ontological substratum of the dominant culture, including some

---

3 The University of Saskatchewan, for example, offers a master's degree cohort in Critical Environmental Education: http://www.usask.ca/education/efdt/critical-enviro-cohort.

of its most deep-seated tenets such as technological optimism, anthropocentrism and subject/object duality. This is what is called for this late in the game, from this deep within the clearcut of anthropogenic climate change and the sixth extinction (Kolbert, 2014); more than eco-friendly lightbulbs, we need to retrofit schools with critical ecological thought.

ॐ

Environmental hermeneutics is an emerging, yet diverse, field and relatively few theorists have delved into the educational implications (for exceptions see D. Smith, 1999; Jardine, 1998; Seidel & Jardine, 2014; Kulnieks et al., 2010). In order to explore some of the connections and contentions between environmental hermeneutics and critical ecohermeneutics, we will look at two visions of "critical" in John van Buren's article "Critical Environmental Hermeneutics" (1995) and David Utsler's article "Paul Ricoeur's Hermeneutics as a Model for Environmental Philosophy" (2009). While neither article explicitly addresses education, there are, I believe, important educational implications implied in each, and my intention is not so much to critique one interpretation over another, but to explore what is called for by critical hermeneutic inquiry in an age of ecological emergency.

John van Buren has written extensively on Heideggerian philosophy and environmental ethics. The critical dimension of environmental hermeneutics, as he construes it in his article, provides a means to philosophically reflect and spell out issues and interest groups involved in forest usage conflicts. In this sense, he focuses on the practical application of hermeneutics to environmental issues in order to address "general features of interpretation, specifically of the environment, and attempts to clarify and help us cope with the epistemological, ethical and political conflicts that arise" (1995, p. 260). Van Buren is a patently adept scholar, and he thoughtfully summarizes a diverse array of interpretations of forests ranging from the lumber company, to the traditional Amerindian experience, and even a bioregional anarchist perspective. And yet, very little in the clean categorizations and heuristic models strikes me as *critical* in terms of challenging the narratives of the dominant culture. Critical, for van Buren, has to do with developing the reflexive capacity required for "arbitrating conflicts" and cultivating "communicative openness in institutional forums for dialogue in which all knowledges, values, and social groups can participate" (pp. 267-268). His proposed forums for dialogue are inspired by the Socratic tradition and the "fundamental social demand" in our civilization for "rationality" and "reasonableness" in our communicative dealings with others.

This, however, begs the question: *why* should we expect such principled dialogue? What historical evidence is there for such a fundamental social demand outside the rhetoric and want of ideal situations? From the critically-minded grassroots, one finds it difficult to expect "rationality" and "reasonableness" in communicative dealings with a colonial-capitalist state founded and maintained on the genocidal suppression of Indigenous peoples and the wholesale destruction of vast tracts of the landscape for short term capital gains (among the legions of other historical and contemporary atrocities committed by North American states—see Zinn, 1999; Alfred, 1999; Kincheloe, 2010; Kahn, 2010; Martusewicz et al., 2011). Or put in different terms to accentuate a hermeneutic point—what comprises a "rational" and "reasonable" response when faced with the systematic exploitation and toxification of one's home? It is, of course, "open to interpretation," but the role of critical ecohermeneutics here is not to "level the field" in order to arbitrate the conflict or provide ethical prescriptions, but rather to create the space for a critical moment whereby dominant narratives are situated within their cultural-historical development and where subaltern, local and more-than-human voices and perspectives become foregrounded as "reasonable." My fear, as exemplified by a new breed of "sensible" neo-environmentalists (Patrick Moore, for example, one of self-proclaimed founders of Greenpeace who has now "dropped out" of "environmental extremism" into reactionary "sensibility"), is that appeals to "rationality" and "reasonableness" easily become apologist logics for sustaining or retrofitting the status quo (Moore, 2014; also see Kingsnorth, 2013). The mythopoetic roots remain.

Another immediate concern is that marginalized experiences, ways of being and relating with the forest simply do not "fit" with institutional forums of dialogue and might easily be written off as "irrational." Van Buren acknowledges more radical "nonanthropocentric egalitarian moralities" such as ecofeminism, biocentrism and green varieties of anarchism, but these positions are ultimately subsumed in his primary categories of human actors related to forest usage, namely: *people, officials,* and *academics* (1995, p. 265). Although van Buren claims that his is a deep hermeneutics, which analyzes the underlying epistemological, ethical and political sense of practices and interpretations of the environment, it rarely, or unsatisfactorily, challenges the substrata of ontological presuppositions informing dominant narratives. While there is absolutely no doubt in my mind that van Buren is well-intentioned, and a part of me wants to believe in his vision of critical hermeneutics as a rational and multiperspectival discourse, when I speak of critical ecohermeneutics, I am speaking less of a set of legitimation criteria to which diverse interest groups could subscribe, and more of a pedagogical strategy aimed at decomposing dominant narratives in order to make space for the possibility of a radically new relational ontology.

On the one hand, a critical ecohermeneutic understanding seeks to draw ways of knowing into an ecology of possibility, for which multivocal interpretation of the kind van Buren is referring to is essential (although extended beyond the horizon of human exceptionalism to more-than-human political agents). On the other hand, it is vital not to succumb to ideological naivete and relativism. Van Buren sees the critical task as one of arbitrating conflicts between different interest group "truth-values," ensuring that conflicts are "addressed in a clear and intelligent manner without the parties involved talking, as they often do, at cross-purposes" (p. 267). The problem is that politics and, for that matter, pedagogy is never so clean and ideal; and while van Buren dreams of these complex, emotion-laden issues being "worked out at the table in rational debate" (p. 268), we must recognize that even the table itself is not culturally neutral or universally appropriate. A critical ecohermeneutic sensibility would never suggest, for example, the Yinka Dene Alliance of First Nations opposing the tarsand pipelines on the west coast of British Columbia be "reasonable" and sit down at the table to "rationally" dialogue like civilized peoples do. This is not what is called for. We are already at cross-purposes, particularly when it comes to ontological presuppositions about "the world." As Bringhurst describes:

> The European colonists' arrival in the New World marks the escalation of a war that had been fought in Europe and Asia for more than two millennia and continues even now. It is a war between those who think they belong to the world and those who think the world belongs to them. It is the war between the pagans, who know they are surrounded and outnumbered by the gods, and all the devotees of the number one—one empire, one history, one market, or one God—and who nowadays insist on the pre-eminence of everyone for himself: the smallest number one of all. (2006, pp. 40-41)

This is not meant as a declaration of eternal conflict, but an ethically motivated opening of the landscape of possibility beyond narrowly defined modes of Western "rationality" and ideal discourse situations. Critical approaches do not entail sitting industrialists, politicians, academics, Indigenous leaders, environmentalists and "the common people" at the same table, as if leveling the playing field in the spirit of communicative rationality might somehow, and in spite of history, lend itself to mutual understanding and radically new ethical imperatives. The premises and the environment itself—the shape of the table, the pens and paper, cameras and lawyers, the stultifying air of the boardroom and styrofoam cups—are already too deeply enmeshed in power relations to simply transcend (Foucault, 1984). Why not meet in a pit-house (assuming one was invited) and tell stories of the ancestors before negotiations? Why not meet in the place slated for destruction itself and allow space for other voices who call this home to enter the dialogue and decision making process? No, this is madness, patently irrational.

Habermas does not surface in the writings of van Buren in any explicit way, but van Buren's "ethical-political norms of communicative environmental reason" (p. 275) seem reminiscent of Habermas's quasi-transcendental principles of communicative reason. I will admit, that while these communicative norms are too ideal and prescriptive for the political arena, there does seem something of value here with respect to the classroom.

> ...this story of communicative discourse, of "getting together and talking things out," is a meta-narrative not in the sense of particular, substantive, and homogenous perspective that ideologically marginalizes all other perspectives, but rather in the sense of a nonsubstantive, procedural narrative that, without falling into subjectivism, makes room for radical heterogeneity and localism in environmental narratives. It espouses coexistence, communication, compromise, cooperation, and consensus. (van Buren, p. 275)

I concede that the communicative approach van Buren outlines here does seem like a sensible approach for classroom discussion; at the very least, we can agree that "getting together and talking things out" is a good starting place for education. But ecological education also calls for something other than "dwelling together with our differences under the same roof" (p. 275). Evoking Heidegger, van Buren has described his environmental communicative discourse as environmental hospitality that opens the doors to rational debate between different environmental knowledges and values. As an ideal, he claims, "environmental communicative reason is a mansion with many rooms" (p. 275). As an opposing metaphor, critical ecohermeneutics also wishes to "open the doors," not to travel from one room to another, but to walk away from the mansion and the schoolhouse and get outside so that we might calibrate our thinking with the ecology of what-is beyond the institutional arrangements of the dominant culture. This is what being *critical* means.

David Utsler (2009) has also briefly sketched some possibilities for critical hermeneutics in environmental discourse. Utsler draws on the work of French philosopher Paul Ricoeur (1991) who, in the tradition of Heidegger and Gadamer, worked to bridge phenomenological description with ontological hermeneutics. Utsler focuses on Ricoeur's "hermeneutics of the self" and the principle of "distanciation"—that interpretation is not about deciphering the intentions of the author but explicating "the type of being-in-the-world unfolded in *front* of the text" (Ricoeur, 1991, p. 86)—as a means of employing Ricoeur in the service of environmental philosophy. While Utsler tends to frame his discussion more in "philosophical" terms than a critical praxis or pedagogy, the challenge to anthropocentrism and the self-constituted subject at the core of his work actually poses a deeper and more *critical* threat to dominant narratives than the critical environmental hermeneutics described by van Buren.

Utsler employs Ricoeur's "hermeneutics of the self" as a means to rethink the anthropocentrism of the dominant culture, as well as the equally problematic and dualistic ecocentrism of some ecologically minded theorists and activists, in order to cultivate the grounds for an "environmental identity" that acknowledges ecological co-constitutionality.

> The self, in Ricoeur's philosophy, is not a self-constituting, immediate subject, but is, in part, constituted by the other. Self-understanding comes by way of a reflective, analytical detour and the dialectic of the self and the other-than-self over against the immediate positing of the subject in the cogito. Thus, a hermeneutics of the self as an account of personal identity would not oppose the anthropocentric to the ecocentric, but would actually require a creative tension between both to develop what I call "environmental identity"—i.e., self-understanding in relation to the environment. Neither the ecocentric self nor the anthropocentric self is privileged over the other; rather each is a constitutive element of one's identity.... Whereas at first glance, anthropocentrism and ecocentrism would appear to create a conflict of interpretations, a Ricoeurian hermeneutics of self mediates the two toward a more robust understanding of the self and the relation to nature. (p. 174)

This Ricoeurian dialectic between self and other is not, as Utlser maintains, merely comparative or superficial; the dialectic is such that, "the selfhood of oneself implies otherness to such an intimate degree that one cannot be thought of without the other, that instead one passes into the other" (Ricoeur, 1992, p. 3). The deep "intercorporeal relationship" that Utsler describes between human and world is, in essence, similar to ecological readings of Merleau-Ponty's "flesh"

(Abram, 1996) and the Heidegger-inspired notion of eco-constitutionality described previously in chapter five. The ethical and pedagogical implications are such that mere rational debates about the values and norms applied to environmental issues by various interest groups as something "out there" are unsatisfactory. We are already *within* the ecological crisis, its origins and effects are already inside us. The crisis is as much one of ontological presuppositions regarding what comprises the self (or "rationality" for that matter) as it is a crisis regarding natural resource mismanagement or what comprises sustainable development. Environmental education, therefore, must entail critical ontological inquiries into the nature of self and otherness in order to come to a more robust understanding and ethics informed by intercorporeality. As Utsler has written, "Consideration of the tapestry of ecological relationships, including the human threads within, reveals a way in which we can come to think of the environment as another self based on intercorporeality. We may begin to understand the self so that it cannot be thought of without the Other of the natural world" (p. 175). To know that *this* man who is hungry or thirsty, or *this* fistful of red maple leaves, *this* bird, *this* tree, *this* perfect circle of mushrooms, really exists as much as I do—that is enough, the rest follows of itself.

Although Utsler's vision of ecohermeneutics accentuates the interwoven tapestry of self and world, it must be noted, he too envisions its practical task as a "starting point for navigating the tension between competing environmental visions and narratives" (p. 175), and in this respect, he is not all that far from van Buren's communicative reason. On the other hand, his emphasis on the critical role of distanciation in Ricoeur's thinking begins to veer towards the possibility of a "critical/hermeneutical environmental philosophy" (p. 177) that is, I believe, more in keeping with the critical task of ecohermeneutic pedagogy. For Ricoeur, distanciation is what allows for the critical moment and essentially describes the critical reflexivity of what, in keeping with my thinking with fungi, I have been calling deliquescence. Here too, critique of ideology is not something that refers only to conditions or abstractions "out there," but comprises a necessary discipline in order to recalibrate self-understanding (Ricoeur, 1991). As Utlser notes, in whatever way we narrate our understanding of ecology and self, "the divergence of interpretations and even the conflict of interpretations of the environment provide a space for critique through which we remain open to new and possible worlds" (p. 176). The critical task of ecohermeneutics is providing the space for such possibilities and while van Buren, Utsler, and I have not sufficiently developed the means to address the political agency of more-than-human actors, one can hear the beginnings of that possibility:

> The critical moment is not only useful within the confines of environmental philosophy and its varying viewpoints and debates. It is likewise a useful analytical tool in the social and political realms where environmental policy is made. Here we must expand the "critical moment" to the notion of a critical hermeneutics. Hermeneutics, according to Ricoeur, takes into account the historical conditions that shape our understanding, bound up with our own finitude. Critical theory, or the critique of ideology, makes judgments that concern distortions in communication revealing domination and oppression, and presses for genuine liberation and freedom. A critical environmental hermeneutics, therefore, considers the conditions within which we interpret the environment while at the same time seeks to uncover distortions in interpretation as well as distortions of communicative environmental rationality—i.e., the discourse we can have with non-human others. (p. 177).

Dig your hands into the soil. Wait. Leave them—on the phenomenological edge—working through a lifetime of being told earth is *dirty* (meaning "smutty, morally unclean" from the 1590s), *filthy* (meaning "physically unclean, dirty, noisome" from the late 14th century), and *profane* (from Latin *profanus* "unholy, not consecrated," and from *pro fano* "not admitted into the temple (with the initiates)" and literally "out in front of the temple"). Wait. *To repeat: don't think, but look!*

Ivan Illich: "Look down at soil, humbly. Search below our feet because our generation has lost its grounding in both soil and virtue" (as cited in Prakash, 2009).

Ah, flesh.
A critical moment.

chapter eight

re-indigenization & the ethics of home-making

If the root metaphors of modernism—individualism, anthropocentrism, faith in progress—help us understand the ideological origins of pre-ecological thinking, the cultural construct of "colonization" can help us to understand how those assumptions have been expressed in geopolitical practices that impact people and places everywhere. If cultural studies in education are to be rooted in historical and geographical reality, they need somehow to confront the fact that underneath the story of progress and economic development (which undergirds the story of schooling) is the story of colonization. (Greenwood, 2013, p. 285)

"If this is your land," he asked, "where are your stories?" (Gitksan elder as cited in Chamberlin, 2003, p. 1)

In chapter four we briefly touched on the work of Andrejs Kulnieks, Dan Roronhiake:wen Longboat, and Kelly Young (2010) to get a sense of some of the possible features of an ecohermeneutic curriculum on the ground. In this chapter I would like to return to that curricular vision to parse out some of the specifics and reconsider what it means to conceive of ecohermeneutics as "re-indigenization" in a colonial state. Some of the key curricular features we will address are: connection to an "ecojustice framework," the ecological significance of oral traditions and Indigenous ways of knowing, and the cultivation of a deep and storied relation with place. Following this overview we will examine the threat of colonial appropriation of "re-indigenization" in light of, what I consider, shallow and expedient moves by the British Columbia

Ministry of Education to incorporate "Traditional Ecological Knowledge and Wisdom" into the present structure of school without paying heed to living Indigenous peoples or the methodologies and forms of education appropriate to engendering Indigenous ways of knowing. I will conclude by exploring the potential of a curriculum sensibility called "Indigenous Metissage" as a way to respectfully, humbly and critically reimagine ecohermeneutics as a pedagogy of decolonization that necessitates the clearing of an "ethical space" between Indigenous peoples and Canadian settlers (Donald, 2009).

ॐ

The ecohermeneutic vision of curriculum outlined by Kulnieks et al. (2010) is the most compelling design in the current literature and the most consonant with the critical ecohermeneutic approach proposed in this book. Its key features are as follows:

- cultivating awareness of place, history and culture through storytelling
- acknowledging the value of oral traditions and intergenerational knowledges
- utilizing interpretive and experiential learning in the process of inquiry
- incorporating holistic medicines, local foods and ethnobotanical knowledges
- analyzing the cultural roots of the ecological crisis vis-à-vis an ecojustice framework

Before we address the curricular significance of oral traditions, Indigenous knowledges and place, I would like to give a brief overview of ecojustice education and trace some of its natural affinities with ecohermeneutics.

Ecojustice education has provided a critical framework for understanding the connections between cultural ways of knowing, education and the ecological crisis for over thirty years (Bowers, 1993, 1997, 2009; Bowers & Martusewicz, 2004; Martusewicz et al., 2011). Its proponents hold that the ecological crisis is largely the result of cultural myths that pre-date widespread concern about the impacts of human activity (in the Western tradition). Chet Bowers (1997) has described this pre-ecological prejudice as comprised of "root metaphors" that mythopoetically frame "reality" for a given cultural group and from which educational practices ensue.

> According to Bowers, three root metaphors that are expressed in education include hyper-individualism, unbounded faith in progress (especially science and its technologies), and extreme anthropocentrism, or the idea that human interests are all that really matter. From a cultural studies perspective, other guiding metaphors that find expression in education include patriarchy, Whiteness, mechanism, colonization, and other terms describing patterns of domination and control that privilege some social groups at the expense of others and that privilege humans at the expense of habitat. All of these metaphors converge and find expression in the universal call for "economic development."... This tautology is so strong that few educators (even those ostensibly committed to social justice), and even fewer policymakers, question an educational system premised on fostering economic growth. (Greenwood, 2013, p. 283)

An ecojustice approach to curriculum focuses, in part, on enabling critical reflection upon these root metaphors in order to provoke teachers and students to question the taken-for-granted (economic) imperatives and tautologies that underlie modern schooling. The ecohermeneutic task here lies in tracing this reflexive discipline all the way down and situating the ontologics of human exceptionalism as a historically effected consciousness inculcated by various imperial and colonial interests, most recently those under the aegis of "neoliberalism" (Derby et al., 2015). Hyper-individualism, the autonomous self, technological optimism, pious and incorruptible faith in human progress—the critical task of ecologically-minded educators is to provoke recognition of these "root metaphors" as interpolated habits of mind; deep mythopoetic constructs inculcated, in part, but also to a great extent, by an education system geared towards reproducing the colonial logic of dominion over the natural world. It may even be the case that this exploitative human-world logic serves as the humus-leached glebe in which other forms of social injustice take root and become thinkable in the first instance. As Abram has maintained: "...justifications for social exploitation draw their force from the prior hierarchicalization of the natural landscape, from that hierarchical ordering that locates 'humans', by virtue of our incorporeal intellect, above and apart from all other, 'merely corporeal', entities" (1996, p. 48; also see Kahn, 2010; Lewis & Kahn, 2010).

Ecojustice education is committed to supporting community efforts to revitalize their local and vernacular "cultural commons" (intergenerational practices, relations, rituals, policies, languages, etc.). As Kulnieks et al. illustrate, there is a natural affinity between ecojustice education and an ecohermeneutic understanding of curriculum due to mutual respect for oral traditions and Indigenous knowledges to (re-)make and (re-)vitalize the eco-ethical relations that tend to emerge from a vernacular commons attuned with place.

> Developing an ecojustice framework of reconnecting with life-sustaining ecologies of place can provide a much needed opportunity to develop the language required to re-learn and develop human relationships with the land that gives life to the present and future generations. Since ecohermeneutics necessitates storytelling, it is important to develop language that helps learners connect with natural landscapes. An ecojustice framework ultimately supports an ecohermeneutic curriculum by providing a vocabulary for naming the very things that separate humans and the natural world... (2010, p. 21)

While it holds that a vocabulary to name our severances is vital in the development of ecocritical analysis, this does not *necessarily* provide the means to nurture integral, holistic or immersive connections with place. Here we must complement ecocritical consciousness by turning towards ecopoetic methodologies that draw upon the meditational means of oral traditions—myth, metaphor, mystery, play, trick, to name but a few—in order to elicit sensitivity to the resonant relation between place and self. An important aspect of revitalizing the commons thus lies in providing the means to re-learn and cultivate the kinds of poetics and attentive practices that elicit these experiences. In other words, ecohermeneutic pedagogy inoculates the vernacular ecocultural landscape in order to detoxify the soil of essentialist epistemicides and make a home for "indigenous" forms of life to flourish.

ॐ

The pedagogic significance of oral traditions runs deeper, of course, than the recognition that orality precedes literacy in the linear march towards idealized and objective "rationality." Oral kinds of understanding are not to be developed with an eye to the inevitable and more desirable literacy of a "civilized" and "educated" mind. Rather the ways of knowing and making sense that emerge with oral modes of engagement (or what Egan has referred to as "mythic understanding") need to be resituated as robust and revered in their own right; and the "development" between orality and literacy resituated as one of non-linear "gains and losses" (Egan, 1987, 1997). Abram has echoed these sentiments calling attention to the conjunction between a literate Plato employing the new technologies of reading and writing in ancient Greece, and his mostly non-literate teacher Socrates, claiming this "may be the hinge on which the sensuous, mimetic, profoundly embodied style of consciousness proper to orality gave way to the more detached, abstract mode of thinking engendered by alphabetic literacy" (1996, p. 109; also see Havelock, 1986). Abram holds that this move from a sensuous reciprocity with things to abstract detachment, what Alfred

Chapter Eight

North Whitehead has called "the celibacy of the intellect" (as cited in Fox, 1983, p. 23), has grave ecological consequences. Critical ecohermeneutics thus shares with both Abram and Bringhurst when they insist: "*The rejuvenation of oral culture is an ecological imperative*" (Bringhurst, 2006, p. 175, italics in original).

Drawing on the work of Abram and Bringhurst, Kulnieks et al. reiterate the way in which the Western tradition, conditioned long-term by this more detached mode of thinking, has been severed from a sense of the "sonorous presence of Earth spirits" (2010, p. 17). In describing the oral traditions of Indigenous peoples (here specifically in response to a description of the worldview of the "Koyukon Indians" of north central Alaska), Abram claims that the language practices and poetics of oral peoples tend to engender an intrinsically different relation with place:

> The practice of language among indigenous peoples would seem to carry a very different significance than it does in the modern West. Enacted primarily in song, prayer, and story, among oral peoples language functions not simply to dialogue with other humans but also to converse with the more-than-human cosmos, to renew reciprocity with the surrounding powers of earth and sky, to invoke kinship even with those entities which, to the civilized mind, are utterly insentient and inert. (1996, pp. 70-71)

None of this is meant to deride literacy or writing. We cannot simply relinquish the written word; rather, as Abram has claimed, our task as ecological educators is *taking up* the written word and "writing language back into the land" (or, rather, the land back into *language*).

> Our craft is that of releasing the budded, earthly intelligence of our words, freeing them to respond to the speech of the things themselves—to the green uttering-forth of leaves from the spring branches. It is the practice of spinning stories that have the rhythm and lilt of the local soundscape, tales for the tongue, tales that want to be told, again and again, sliding off the digital screen and slipping off the lettered page to inhabit these coastal forests, those desert canyons, those whispering grasslands and valleys and swamps.... Planting words, like seeds, under rocks and fallen logs—letting language take root, once again, in the earthen silence of shadow and bone and leaf. (pp. 273-274)

Similarly, Kulnieks et al. do not see a "hard and fast dichotomy between oral and literary tradition in cultures that employ both as a means of representing knowledge because they can become part of one another" (p. 17). The task in education is thus recognizing the "gains and losses" of each kind of understanding, but *taking up* each as fully as possible as a means of writing, thinking and singing our way towards an ecology of resonance (Lilburn, 2002; Zwicky, 2003; Bringhurst, 2008; Dickinson & Goulet, 2010).

From an ecohermeneutic perspective, *texts are ecological.* "Writing, like human language, is engendered not only within the human community but between the human community and the animate landscape, born of the interplay and contact between the human and the more-than-human world" (Abram, 1996, p. 95). This seemingly self-evident observation (how else could text be?) is, evidently, easily obfuscated by the way textual language itself and conventional education can omit direct interplay and resonance with particular places (Kulnieks et al., 2010, pp. 21–22). It goes without saying that Western education systems are fixated on text and print-centric forms of learning. An ecohermeneutic curriculum works to move beyond strict print-centrism towards experiential, storied and contemplative inquiry *with* place.

> Rather than depending solely upon its reconstruction through print-centered learning, eco-hermeneutics seeks to include interpretive experiential learning in the process of inquiry. These investigations include properly learning to tell and interpret stories that are indigenous to the place they live.... These important interpretive practices involve the exploration of intergenerational knowledge and necessitate that learners become involved in the practices of understanding the ecology of place by developing a relationship with the local places which they inhabit. (pp. 17-18)

This process of inquiry, it must be reiterated, entails more than simply "getting outside" and "telling stories." The story must be, as it were, attuned to place—the imaginative yield of some (often long-term, reiterative and disciplined, and occasionally ritualized and sacred) practice of attending, coupled with much "knowledge," and in the service of "truth-telling."

> Storytelling is at the core of eco-hermeneutic curricula. For example, in Indigenous cultures stories are situated within a particular place which is often connected to natural settings. Stories are corporeal and neurological. Through engagement with human beings, they grow in both meaning and application.... Since Western knowledge has historically been and continues to be privileged in terms of being perceived to be contained within written form, narratives have often been relegated to a source of anecdotal, fictional or fairy tale form. However, in the mid-to-late 20th century, we have seen a shift in the ways that some researchers and scholars address literary tradition by including an emphasis on developing a relationship with place through oral tradition. Both are important components of the educational process...
>
> The Haudenosaunee version of the term story refers to someone speaking their truth, their understanding of or a reflection upon, ancient knowledge truths. In relaying or sharing these truths, the speaker has an accountability to maintaining the integrity

Chapter Eight

of this ancient knowledge. In this way of speaking ancestral knowledge becomes alive, connective and real within the oral traditions of place. (p. 18)

Keeping the ecocritical in mind, this process of inquiry and storytelling must concurrently work on the substratum of the dominant culture to deliquesce privileged habits that are already established. This requires a certain discipline; an understanding of ecological education as an applied practice of hyperactive pessimism (chapter five). This is difficult work, oscillating between the distance required to critique invasive ideologies and the relational intimacy required to recognize what-is, real work (Snyder, 1980).

On the one hand, learning in context and allowing time for experiential interplay and immersion in the natural world will, to a certain, but ultimately limited extent, naturally lend itself to "ecological understanding" (Derby et al., 2013). On the other hand, we *must* be thoughtful in the ways we imaginatively engage students with story and writing, using language that "should be kept in responsive contact with the world of experience, all the way through the process of language development and intellectual growth" (Fettes, 2013, p. 4). Here, working on the level of metaphor *through* writing provides a powerful tool to trace, reflect upon and even provoke resonant encounters. I envision these ecopoetic encounters as a kind of rewilding of literacy (McKay suggests that metaphors are "...entry points where wilderness re-invades language, the place where words put their authority at risk..." [2002, p. 61]). This does not mean the curriculum becomes a tedious reiteration of outdoor poetry sessions (though one might hope for a few), but rather a thoughtful coupling of experiential learning, meaningful narratives and imaginative engagement that lends itself to an earthen cadence in our "school work" (Fettes, 2013; Judson, 2010, 2015; also see Seidel, 2014, for an example in lyric form).

༈

Drinking from a glass half-full, I am confident that there is no lack of concern about ecological issues amongst *most* educators. The question is, what, in practice, should we do if rejuvenating oral culture is indeed an ecological imperative? How do everyday Science, Math, History and English teachers address the complexities of incorporating oral traditions into the very form and structure of school amidst the maelstrom of new ecologically themed curricular addendums, books and documentaries that proliferate on the resource shelf? Is awareness of these global issues not the primary objective of environmental education? Why, as Bringhurst has asked, are oral traditions so important?

> Because oral culture means much more and less than simply talking. Rekindling oral culture means rejoining the community of speaking beings—sandhill cranes, whitebark pines, coyotes, wood frogs, bees and thunder.
>
> Oral culture also means much more than telling stories. It means learning how to hear them, how to nourish them, and how to let them live. It means learning how to let stories swim down in yourself, grow large in there, and rise back up again. It does not—repeat does *not*—mean memorizing the lines so you can act the script you've written or recite the book you've read. Oral culture—and any culture at all—involves, as nature does, a lot of repetition. But rote memorization and oral culture are two very different things.
>
> If you embody an oral culture, you are a working part of a place, a part of the soil in which stories live their lives. There will in that event be stories you know by heart—but when the stories come out of your mouth, as when the trees come out of the ground, no two performances will ever be the same. Each incarnation of a story is itself. (2006, p. 175)

It has been my experience that when *most* people hear one turn to the topic of oral traditions or Indigenous knowledges, they tend to respond with something to the effect of: "yes, that is all well and good, but we cannot go back." This sentiment is problematic on a couple of counts. Firstly, it is clearly enmeshed in the root metaphors of "progress" and "development" as well as a modern Western sense of the linear geometry of time. While the notion of progress has been much maligned in recent decades with the advent of postmodernist thought (Usher & Edwards, 1994) and the mainstreaming of ecological limitations and catastrophes (McKibben, 1999; Wright, 2004; Shiva, 2005; Kolbert, 2014), there remains a strong sense that time is still somehow carrying us "forward," and that we cannot "go back." This delusion is, of course, propelled by some of the other mythopoetics of modernity, specifically technological optimism; and while an in-depth discussion of the phenomenology of time is beyond the scope of this book, suffice to say, from an ecohermeneutic perspective, we cannot "go forward" either. There is nowhere to go but here. Or as Bringhurst has starkly put it: "There are no new worlds. Paradise will not be our asylum, and hell will not be anywhere other than here" (2006, p. 45). The notion that we cannot revitalize and re-learn knowledges, conventions, social arrangements and ontological relations from the past because this is not in line with our programme of "progress," or that ancient wisdom has nothing to teach the modern world (Davis, 2009), is preposterous and fundamentally anti-hermeneutic.

Secondly, there is an inherent political defeatism at the core of such sentiments (reminiscent of Heidegger's surrender to the logic of machination—see chapter five) implying that this "progressive" march is inevitable, come hell or high water, as it were. This is less a philosophical or pedagogical position and more an ill-considered capitulation to the drone of neoliberal rhetoric. I wonder if shifting the metaphor might help? While it is true, in a certain, but very real sense, we can never "go back" linearly—just as we can never "go back" linearly from literacy to orality, or "go back" in material time from a state of ecological degradation to the relative biodiversity of "pre-contact America"—surely we can "return," as in re-orient, as in turn towards. The cultural myth of being permanently expelled from "Eden" (read: intimate and sensuous relation with the more-than-human cosmos) and having to look ever skywards, forwards and "outside" in order to transcend this condemned flesh has obvious origins that have been, to put it lightly, hypostatized beyond resonance or relevance. Towards the end of his life, Gregory Bateson put this insight in no uncertain terms:

> If you put God outside and set him vis-à-vis his creation, and if you have the idea that you are created in his image, you will logically and naturally see yourself as outside and against the things around you. And as you arrogate all mind to yourself, you will see the world around you as mindless and therefore not entitled to moral or ethical consideration. The environment will seem to be yours to exploit. Your survival unit will be you and your folks or conspecifics against the environment of other social units, other races and the brutes and vegetables.
>
> If this is your estimate of your relations to nature AND YOU HAVE AN ADVANCED TECHNOLOGY, your likelihood of survival will be that of a snowball in hell. You will die either of the toxic byproducts of your own hate, or, simply, of overpopulation and overgrazing. (1972, p. 468)

Conversely, the ecohermeneutic mind—shaped as it is by oral modes of consciousness—draws attention "down" towards the moist and fleshy earth of participatory reciprocity (Abram, 1996). Here—hands buried in the soil—the geometry of time is recyclical, seasonal, iterative, a vortex of now. Those who speak of returning to oral traditions are rarely suggesting we "go back" in some linear sense, rather what they are trying to get at is a deep sense of being here (and being *of* here) as an ever-present ontological possibility. "A bridge," as Gadamer likened it, "built between the once and the now" (1976, p. 22).

The revitalizations of oral traditions and Indigenous knowledges are ecological concerns because they offer a means of *return* to the community of speaking beings. An ecohermeneutic curriculum is aimed at rekindling oral culture—not simply more talking, or teaching as telling more stories, or evoking more discussion about "environmental issues" (in fact, in a certain sense, it is a recognition of the pedagogic significance of ineffability and silence)—but learning how to listen to the voice of the other and enter into relation with particular places as embodied and participatory curricular inquiries. Listening as a way of learning to *be* (*Bildung* in resonance with *physis*—see chapter six). The relational ontology at its heart bears inherent ethical implications in how one *walks* in the world. Our *real* ecological footprint as it were, not measured in carbon impact or sequestration, but wisdom. As Saulteaux (Anishinaabe) scholar L. Akan (as cited in Kulnieks) has written:

> The Elders' "walk talks" help us not to "walk around blind" or not to be in ignorance. This involves being mindful, to be aware of ourselves, conscientious of our actions and other living things...it involves knowing our epistemology, our ontology and our cosmology. (as cited in Kulnieks et al., 2010, p. 17)

Kulnieks et al. further emphasize the "everyday" (read: epistemological, ontological, cosmological) dimensions of ecological education, drawing place-based connections between eating and knowing: "As with food, it is clear that stories come from a particular place" (p. 19); and healing and knowing, "Another important connection between story and place and spirit involves food and medicine as they give us life and for this reason the way we should behave in relation to that place is a sacred one" (p. 19). Walking, eating, speaking, listening, singing, knowing, healing—each gesture a manifestation of a particular worldview, each a potentially fecund place-based pedagogical moment.

ॐ

Ecohermeneutic curriculum as re-indigenization is a conceptualization that, I suspect, would find much support from radical ecological educators who understand and are committed to education as a means of cultural transformation, but I wonder how it might land with Indigenous scholars, educators, activists, and communities? What are the implications of proposing re-indigenization in a colonial state such as Canada that has utilized, and continues to utilize, its educational system as a means of genocide and political suppression? As a first-generation Irish settler, born on the traditional territories of the K'omox and currently occupying unceded Coast Salish territory (specifically Musqueam, Squamish and Tsleil-Waututh), the whole proposition is fraught with complexities and trepidations. What exactly does *re-indigenization* mean? How, for example, do we navigate the difference between *indigenizing*

Chapter Eight

culture and *being Indigenous*? Ecohermeneutic educators must remain critically minded and careful that we do not collapse the subtle but important difference between "oral traditions"—which are, in a sense, universal—and "Indigenous knowledges"—which are the living manifestations of Indigenous peoples of particular places. After all, everyone is *not*, as the crass liberal adage goes, indigenous to somewhere. We, and here I speak of non-Indigenous peoples in Canada, are settlers here, despite the fact we too call this place home, and any project of home-making must emerge from an ethical space of profound humility.

ॐ

> The educator who sees education as culturally neutral is similar to the spouse of an alcoholic who denies the alcoholism. There are implications for practice, self-concept, and feelings that both are unable to face. Perverse ignorance is a particular form of the defence mechanism of denial.... It is understandable that the educator with a self-concept tied to the ideal of helping children, with preparation that does not include multicultural competence, with a curriculum that ignores or systematically distorts the culture of his or her students, and with unresolved personal issues of racism and ethnocentrism could not recognize the extent to which education is both culturally bound and actively hostile to Native culture. (Hampton, 1995, p. 36)

> Adding a sprinkling of our culture to European parasitic culture is offensive, particularly in the absence of an understanding of our laws and the philosophy that underlies them. To spice the ideology of exploitation, individualism and middle-class aspiration with the emptied art-forms and stripped songs of the ancients, is to reduce ourselves to a joke. Tradition is useful only insofar as it allows us to continue to make use of our history. (Maracle, 1996, p. 89)

What Chickasaw scholar Eber Hampton and Stó:lō scholar Lee Maracle draw attention to with these stark observations are some of the all-too-common, yet immensely deleterious presuppositions about "education" as a root metaphor tied up with "progress" and "emancipation" in Western thought. Although this book is concerned with education as a means of inoculating Western thinking with spores of ecological consciousness, to misconstrue education as a culturally neutral or a universal panacea to socio-ecological ills is to invisibilize the Indigenous experience and divorce pedagogy from *this* place (again).[1] For

---

[1] As Ivan Illich has written: "Our colleagues are unwilling to recognize that education is a concept...inconceivable in other societies.... They assume the need for education as

many Indigenous peoples the very edifice of education is oppressive, "Western education is hostile in its structure, its curriculum, its context and its personnel" (Hampton, 1995, p. 37). Maracle has stated unequivocally, "Schools have shown themselves to be ideological processing plants, turning out young people who cannot produce the means to sustain themselves, but who are full of the ideological nonsense of European culture" (1996, p. 88).

Despite decades of open hostility, state-sanctioned genocide and egregious abuse by the Canadian educational system, there are still relatively few Indigenous peoples that would prefer a segregated school system (Hampton, 1995, p. 7). Maracle explains, "Segregated schools alone will not change the basic historical pattern of colonialism; only decolonization will do that" (1996, p. 89). Consequently, if ecohermeneutics is aimed at re-indigenizing curriculum, then it must be understood and enacted as a pedagogy of decolonization. As Papaschase Cree educational theorist Dwayne Donald has written, "One of the central curricular and pedagogical challenges of decolonization is to contest the assumption that the historical experiences and perspectives of Aboriginal peoples in Canada are their own separate cultural preoccupations" (2009, p. 6). This is not to recapitulate the claim that "everyone is indigenous to somewhere," which is to say everyone is indigenous to somewhere therefore settlers are free to naturalize to this place. Rather, it is an attempt to recognize the relation between place, knowing and being and *return* Western thinking towards place-based consciousness as an ethical project between nations with a complex colonial past.

Despite our "shared" historical experience, it is crucial that non-Indigenous peoples not lay claim to *being Indigenous* to this land, no matter how many (relatively few) generations their families have been in Canada. Ironically, the first step towards re-indigenization for many may involve honestly acknowledging our essential *non-Indigeneity*. As educational philosopher Derek Rasmussen has asked: "What makes our society non-Indigenous? Why do we in the dominant society refuse to face our non-Indigeneity?"

> An Indigenous people are those who believe that they belong to a place; a non-Indigenous people are those who believe that places belong to them... an honest appraisal says that we non-Indigenous folks have little or no sense of long-term belonging to this land.... We are non-Indigenous because we don't belong anywhere yet. Belonging has

an a-historical given.... Wherever the historian of education finds a poetry ritual, an apprenticeship, an organized game, he smells educational activity" (as cited in Rasmussen, 2011, p. 22).

not soaked into our bones and myths. We still set our course by following the Empire's markers. As a result we have almost no stories that weave us into this landscape. (2011, pp. 28-29)

This point is perhaps best illustrated by a story:

> It happened at a meeting between an Indian community in northwest British Columbia and some government officials. The officials claimed the land for the government. The natives were astonished by the claim. They couldn't understand what these relative newcomers were talking about. Finally one of the elders put what was bothering them in the form of a question. "If this is your land," he asked, "where are your stories?" He spoke in English, but then he moved into Gitksan, the Tsimshian language of his people—and he told a story.
> All of a sudden everyone understood...even though the government foresters didn't know a word of Gitksan, and neither did some of his Gitksan companions. But what they understood was more important: how stories give meaning and value to the places we call home; how they bring us close to the world we live in by taking us into a world of words; how they hold us together and at the same time keep us apart. They also understood the importance of the Gitksan language, especially to those who do not speak it. (Chamberlin, 2003, p. 1)

But while acknowledging non-Indigeneity is an important piece, the other aspect, emphasized in the work of Donald (2009) is the fact that Indigenous culture, traditions and presence have co-constituted "Canadian" society. Now there is difficult, but important work to do.

৯

An ecohermeneutic approach to education *here* (on unceded Coast Salish territory) is synonymous with Indigenous political solidarity and decolonization; and in this sense the projects of revitalizing Indigenous epistemologies, rejuvenating oral traditions in education as an ecological imperative and returning towards place-based consciousness are all threads in the same intertwined undertaking. But the word *decolonization*, like the word *ecological* or *community*, has become troublingly over-mined these days, too often employed as a non-specific panacea to a vast array of social and ecological problems or misappropriated by corporate interests (Tuck & Yang, 2012). How are vastly different cultural ways of knowing and being to occupy the same space? How are we to critically examine the deep (and often aggressively univocal) presuppositions of settler culture? How do settler peoples honestly step back to recognize our essential non-Indigeneity, while reaching open hands in front of us to embrace a place-based relational ontology and the ethical implications thereof?

As we have seen throughout this book, ecocritical discourse analysis is a powerful analytic tool, but perhaps too removed to provoke the kinds of deep relational understandings that emerge primarily from sharing stories, myths, songs, crafts, rituals, space. Perhaps we might approach the process of understanding and healing between Indigenous and non-Indigenous as a kind of ecohermeneutic intertwining—as a process of braiding in the spirit of "ethical relationality."

As a curriculum sensibility this has been called "Indigenous Metissage," which Donald (2009) defines as a place-based and interpretive approach to curriculum informed by an ecological and relational understanding of the world. It is offered as a way to decolonize educational approaches that are tacitly embedded within "colonial frontier logics." For example, by pointing to the fort as a mythic symbol within the Canadian national narrative, Donald illustrates how curricular and pedagogical approaches often reinforce colonial logics and perpetuate the enduring message that Indigenous peoples and Canadian settlers "occupy separate realities." As he has maintained, "The stories told to children in schools about Aboriginal peoples have been largely based on a Eurowestern theory of primitivism that unilaterally places Indigenousness outside comprehension and acknowledgment" (p. 18).

These "colonial frontier logics" are, of course, modern manifestations of preceding cultural imperatives that negate experiences that do not empirically "fit" into the epistemology of Eurowestern modernity (Battiste, 2013; also see Plumwood, 1993 for a strikingly similar reading from an ecofeminist perspective). As living memory of the carnage, obscenity and unapologetic imperialism of the "historical genocide" of Indigenous peoples fades, the colonial project mutates and manifests subtler forms of "hegemonic genocide." Outwardly racist assertions about Indigenous peoples are now increasingly rare (in the limited sense of what is appropriate for public discourse; racism towards Indigenous peoples, of course, remains prevalent and systemic), but the genocidal impetus remains in the infantilization and irrationalization of Indigenous ways of knowing. This has the dual effect of aiding in the continued assimilation and economization of Indigenous peoples, while concurrently preventing the "indigenization" of settlers and thus any widespread or deep solidarity with Indigenous peoples via a "shared" place-based consciousness.[2] The modern education system, as Donald

---

2 For some fascinating accounts of Western colonials "rocking the freshly laid colonial foundations of North America," see Ron Sakolsky and James Koehnline: *Gone to Croatan:*

illustrates, reproduces the colonial logic of unknowability. Both Indigenous peoples and resonant experiences of place are kept as separate realities and viewed as somewhat archaic, inane and primitive. In other words, the relational logic of oral traditions and the knowledges of living Indigenous peoples are both deliberately distorted by Eurowestern narratives steeped in racism and the logic of dominion, so that they seem beyond rational comprehension in the "modern" world for both Indigenous and non-Indigenous peoples alike.

২

Despite the fact that provincial governments across Canada have introduced policy shifts in curricula requiring "meaningful consideration and exploration of Aboriginal perspectives across subject areas" (Donald, 2009, p. 6), this all-too-often results in a "tipis and costumes approach" that is nothing more than a token "sprinkling" of Western curriculum with the "emptied art-forms and stripped songs of the ancients." As Maracle (1996) has insisted, what is absent is a genuine understanding of Indigenous laws and the philosophy that underlies them. Before this "remedial" gesture, however, there must first be a willingness to recognize the history of our relations and return the critically self-reflexive gaze towards Eurowestern modernity. We must first be willing to deliquesce some of our rigid epistemic certainties.

But how are teachers to confront such a violent and unpleasant history of colonial relations with Indigenous peoples, not to mention the continuation of this process in contemporary politics (Alfred, 1999, 2005)? As Donald has written, teachers naturally find it difficult to relinquish the "more comfortable stories of Canada that they have been told and grown accustomed to telling." And asks: "On what terms should this re-reading and reframing be done?" (p. 4).

> To help with rereading, reframing, and reimagining the relationships connecting Aboriginal peoples and Canadians, and thus facilitate the decolonization process in educational contexts, I suggest a curriculum sensibility termed *Indigenous Metissage*. Indigenous Metissage is a research sensibility that imagines curriculum and pedagogy together as a relational, interferential, and hermeneutic endeavour. Doing Indigenous

---

Origins of North American Dropout Culture (Eds., 1993). These accounts do not simply represent early forms of escapism or "going native," but challenge the then newly constructed boundaries between wilderness and civilization. As Sakolsky and Koehnline have written, "This is no mean feat. If we can question the division of our world into the categories of 'civilization' and 'barbarism', then we have begun to question all forms of hierarchy" (1993, p. 9).

> Metissage involves the purposeful juxtaposition of mythic historical perspectives (often framed as commonsense) with Aboriginal historical perspectives. The ethical desire is to reread and reframe historical understanding in ways that cause readers to question their own assumptions and prejudices as limited and limiting, and thus foster a renewed openness to the possibility of broader and deeper understandings that can transverse perceived cultural, civilizational, and temporal divides. One central goal of doing Indigenous Metissage is to promote ethical relationality as a curricular and pedagogical standpoint. Ethical relationality is an ecological understanding of human relationality that does not deny difference, but rather seeks to more deeply understand how our different histories and experiences position us in relation to each other. This form of relationality is ethical because it does not overlook or invisibilize the particular historical, cultural, and social contexts from which a particular person understands and experiences living in the world. It puts these considerations at the forefront of engagements across frontiers of difference. (pp. 5-6)

Engaging across frontiers of difference in the spirit of ethical relationality is a fundamentally different approach than incorporating Aboriginal content, or "Traditional Ecological Knowledge and Wisdom," across the curriculum.

By way of illustration, in the BC Science 10 Integrated Resource Package, under the heading *Aboriginal Content in the Science Curriculum*, we find the following definition:

> Traditional Ecological Knowledge and Wisdom (TEKW) is defined as the study of systems of knowledge developed by a given culture. It brings the concept of wisdom to our discussion of science and technology. TEKW tends to be holistic, viewing the world as an interconnected whole where humans are not regarded as more important than nature. It is a subset of traditional science, and is considered a branch of biological and ecological science. This knowledge with its characteristic respect for sustaining community and environment offers proven conceptual approaches which are becoming increasingly important to all BC residents.
>
> Examples of TEKW science may be accessed through living elders and specialists of various kinds or found in the literature of TEKW, anthropology, ethnology, ecology, biology, botany, ethnobiology, medicine, horticulture, agriculture, astronomy, geology, climatology, architecture, navigation, natural science, engineering, and mathematics.
>
> In British Columbia, the report of the scientific panel for sustainable forest practices in Clayoquot Sound emphasizes TEKW and the importance of including indigenous knowledge in planning and managing traditional territories. (2008, p. 14)

This oddly-worded, obfuscating and calculated bit of political manoeuvring succeeds in ostensibly sounding...eco-friendly. But careful ecocritical examination of the subtle language reveals the troubling persistence of a deep colonial logic. Despite the surface challenge to human exceptionalism and lip service to Indigenous knowledge (in the service of resource management), the authority of Eurowestern modernity as a way of knowing remains beyond question: the inevitability of technology and its patent compatibility with wisdom, traditional knowledge as a "subset" of the sciences, specialization, individualism, discourses of sustainability, discourses of resource management, etc. The convoluted "sprinkling" of this logic with ecological tropes such as *traditional, wisdom, holistic, interconnected, elders, sustainable* and the invoking of environmental consciousness associated with Clayoquot Sound only works to further conceal its colonial underpinning by reframing the sciences as culturally neutral and progressive. A detailed ecocritical analysis is too protracted for this book, but I will discuss a few of the colonial aspects in greater detail.

Firstly, although situated beneath the heading "Aboriginal Content," the term TEKW is conspicuously vague and does not necessarily indicate nor pay proper respect to particular, living Indigenous peoples nor the Indigenous wisdom traditions of particular places in "British Columbia." This is further exacerbated by its definition as a study of systems of knowledge developed by a "given culture." The implied capacity of any "given culture" to develop ecological knowledge and wisdom overlooks, invisibilizes and decontextualizes the particular historical, cultural, and social matrix unique to the Indigenous peoples of *this* place. It also very subtly implies—again, in the tradition that "we are all indigenous to somewhere"—that any "given culture" might naturalize here, developing its own traditional and ecological wisdom as something like "proven conceptual approaches" to sustainable resource management.

Secondly, the inclusion of TEKW allegedly brings "the concept of wisdom to our discussion of science and technology." The critical mind reels at the ostensible ease with which Science 10 teachers in BC are supposed to integrate modern Western scientific concepts with the non-specific and vast "wisdom" of, what exactly, "Aboriginal peoples"—all of them? What, in addition, does "wisdom" imply here—rationality, an ethical reflexivity, an awareness of human limitations? Apparently these scientist-anthropologist-philosopher-king educators attended a different Post Degree Professional Program for teacher training than the one I attended, where Indigenous issues were all but absent. Beyond this inconvenience, there is the underlying assumption that traditional and ecological wisdom, in order to be valid, must be complementary, compatible and in alignment with the trajectory of Eurowestern science and technology. This notion makes little sense unless one construes science, education and technology as culturally neutral, an inherently colonial logic that, as Hampton has established, is a form of "perverse ignorance" and a "defense mechanism of denial." The effect, if not deliberate intent, of calling TEKW a "subset of traditional science" and "a branch of biological and ecological science" is to appropriate difference into the Western canon of sense-making. From an ecohermeneutic perspective, Indigenous epistemologies are not subsets or stepping-stones to more literate, scientific, or civilized ways of knowing. Colonial attempts at conflating ecological sciences with Indigenous epistemologies downplay the ontological incompatibility of those who believe they belong to place and those who believe place belongs to them.

Although examples of TEKW are acknowledged to be accessible through "living elders," this token mention is belittled by the bulk of the statement which champions the knowledge held by "specialists," "literature" and an absurdly generalized list of Western academic disciplines, many of which have been instrumental in perpetuating colonialism in the first place (i.e. anthropology, agriculture, biology, etc.). Here the superiority and universal accessibility of scientific ways of knowing are fundamentally reaffirmed, just in time to "save" educators from the potential discomfort, time input and trouble of forging a relation with a "living elder." Why go to the trouble to develop a relationship with an elder and have her come to speak when you can easily access TEKW via an on-line engineering forum? The particular wisdoms of living Indigenous peoples and traditions as embedded in particular places are thus distorted and replaced by an ethos of equal access to ecological wisdom via specialists and print-centric literature.

The last excerpt of the definition is perhaps the most troubling and the most telling. A resourcist relation with the natural world is clearly evoked with verbs like "planning" and "managing" for "sustainable forest practices," as is the capitalist discourse that underlies sustainability in general. The statement discusses the patent importance of including indigenous knowledge in planning and managing "traditional territories." Is this implying that Indigenous peoples need to employ more managerial skill when extracting resources from the few "traditional territories" they have been accorded by a colonial government? Or is it implying that all of "British Columbia" is now somehow "traditional territory" and that government officials should include some Native drumming or wear some feathers or something (or at least donate some money for a "cultural center") before using the legislature to pave the way for energy corporations to work on contested and unceded land? Despite employing a volley of catchy eco-friendly key words and confusing mixed messages, the inclusion of TEKW in the BC Curriculum is a far cry from engaging with frontiers of difference with ethical relationality. Rather it is indicative of the guileful adaptations and

Chapter Eight

mutations a colonial logic will undergo in order to maintain hegemonic negation of Indigenous peoples as political sovereigns and of the relational ontology that informs Indigenous ways of knowing.

ॐ

Despite the beguiling stratagems and structures of colonial hegemony in Canada, Indigenous Metissage (Donald, 2009; also see Chambers, Hasebe-Ludt, Donald, Hurren, Leggo & Oberg, 2008; Kelly, 2012) offers a means to reread, reframe and reimagine ecohermeneutics as a critical pedagogy of place that thoughtfully enacts the commensurate projects of decolonization and reinhabitation (Gruenewald, 2003)—or in terms of philosophic mycorestoration, the confluent deliquescence and remediation of the colonized landscape. While curricular policies in Canadian schools have acknowledged the importance of "incorporating Aboriginal content," the convoluted language, circumspect modifications and refusal to engage in critical self-reflexivity are cause for suspicion. The move to assimilate Indigenous knowledges into subsets of scientific inquiry in a political-historical vacuum and as culturally neutral, strike more like a calculated colonial gambit, than an authentic gesture of mutual respect. As Donald has written, our relationships are "deeply rooted in colonial processes," and ecological education must therefore be understood as making an ethical space to recycle prejudices and question the limitations of our historical horizons. Rather than invisibilizing or subsuming Indigenous ways of knowing, an ecohermeneutic approach seeks to foreground epistemic diversity and foster openness to the possibilities of being by engaging with difference.

> Through the reciprocal process of teaching and learning, we move closer together. This movement towards holistic intereferentiality and recognition of difference has resonances with ecological understandings of the earth that are antithetical to the teleologics currently shaping the habits and priorities of Homo Oeconomicus. Universalized market logics that seemingly justify intensified resource exploitation and voracious consumerism are indeed deeply connected to the violence—epistemic, institutional, and otherwise—that has been committed in accordance with fort teachings. It is the denial of connectivity that allows such violence and exploitation to continue. I am convinced that we require a new or renewed ethical framework that clarifies the terms by which we can speak to each other about these pressing issues of shared concern. This is the visionary spirit and intent of Indigenous Metissage. (Donald, 2009, p. 18)

Colonization is not a definitive historical event. It is an on-going, syncretic and adaptive project of power that manifests as teleologics of economic rationalism, or the seeming incomprehensibility of the wild and savage other, or in the enduring image of the fort in education as a symbol of national identity and pride. While the oppressive effects of colonial-market logics are unequally distributed and impact Indigenous peoples most severely, colonization is, in a sense, a malignant force doing violence to all of us down-to-earth folk and our more-than-human kin. Donald: "If colonialism is indeed a shared condition, then decolonization needs to be a shared endeavor. I am convinced that decolonization in the Canadian context can only occur when Aboriginal peoples and Canadians face each other across historic divides, deconstruct their shared past, and engage critically with the realization that their present and future are similarly tied together" (2009, p. 5).

chapter nine

conclusion: a tree of meaning

> Mycelium, constantly on the move, can travel across landscapes up to several inches a day to weave a living network over the land. (Stamets, 2005, p. 1)

> ...Merleau-Ponty comes in his final writing to affirm that it is first the sensuous, perceptual world that is relational and weblike in character, and hence that the organic, interconnected structure of any language is an extension or echo of the deeply interconnected matrix of sensorial reality itself. Ultimately, it is not human language that is primary, but rather the sensuous, perceptual life-world, whose wild, participatory logic ramifies and elaborates itself in language. (Abram, 1996, p. 84)

I wanted this book to *move* differently—with some of the wild participatory logic of a mycelial mind—in order that we might come together to recognize the pedagogic significance of the living matrix *beneath* our thinking and being (and beyond our wanting and doing). Echoes of this polyphonic structure reverberate inside us when we think intensely and beautifully; when it gets into our mouths we call it poetry; when it guides how we walk in the world we call it integrity; when we trace its address as a teaching we call it wisdom; when we eat according to it we feel healthy, good, full of truth.

> The intuition of resonant relation is the experience of meaning.

> Which is not to say that we always experience meaning when we use language, or think. It is possible to use words or signs, and to manipulate nonverbal concepts or images, without experiencing their meaning. We often use the word 'mechanical' to describe this kind of speech or thought.

> When attempting to say what an experience of meaning was an experience *of*, on the other hand, we sometimes reach for one or more of the following words: 'truth,' 'beauty,' goodness,' integrity.' (Zwicky, 2003, p. L49)

I wanted these words—coarse and besmirched as they are—to approach you; to reach for you with hands filthy from digging for roots, but from pausing too—hands in the soil—to listen and look. *Here.* This is what I found.

ঽ

Critical ecohermeneutics seeks to join with other ecocritical strategies to inoculate the ecologically destructive presuppositions of the dominant culture, deliquescing the historical privilege and rigidity of epistemic certainties and colonial logics, and mycoremediating the landscape of existential possibility. Specifically, it seeks to guide attunement to meaning as a resonant ecology—the live, metaphorical relation between things and the living, vibrant matrix of what-is (Zwicky, 2003)—in the face of spectacular distractions, distortions, illusions, ideologies, and root metaphors that all converge in education. Its critical task is working on the level of metaphor—at the mythopoetic roots that sustain and inform ontological understanding—by taking up the attentive disciplines and poetics of oral traditions and rewilding literacy as a means of *returning* writing, speaking, singing, crafting and learning towards more-than-human kinship.

While the hermeneutic tradition has been, in a limited and artificially static sense, bound by the ontological horizon of its historical emergence, Gadamer's project has always been one of explicating our prejudices to emphasize the fluidity of being and bringing traditions to bear on our lives as they are lived. In this sense, it is only natural at this historical moment, that hermeneutics go ecological and be brought to bear on the world as an ecopoetic and critical pedagogy of place (Gruenewald, 2003). As Jardine has illustrated, hermeneutics provides a critique of how (environmental) education has become spellbound by weak and intellectually dull-minded versions of the methodologies of the natural sciences (2006, p. 274). These methods of severance, he argues, gut the imaginative familiarity and playful kinship with things that lie at the heart of education as an earthly undertaking. Or in other words, these methods distort the intuition of resonant relation as a kind of *domestic* wisdom.

> This is a fascinating process to which we subject both the instance and ourselves.... Regarding the instance itself, ambiguous linkages and telltale signs and marks of potentially violating interconnectedness are systematically eliminated, producing a sort

> of virginal, untouched instance. And regarding ourselves, we can no longer approach this instance with the moist and fleshy and playful and imaginative familiarity with which we began.... We must remain strictly within the parameters of the methods of severance we have enacted, for any other interconnection would despoil or defile the instance we have so carefully and methodically isolated and purified. Our connection to this instance thus becomes gutted. We understand it "from the neck up" and only within the bounds that our severing and isolating methodology allows. We deny that it is our kin. (p. 275)

Critical ecohermeneutics has thus been construed as a kind of ecopoetic understanding of education in order to restore to pedagogy the wisdom of phenomenological description and imaginative encirclement when attuned with ecological form. This is a *critical* discipline, as Zwicky has reminded us: "... one's preference for a style of explanation will depend on one's purposes. (Just don't imagine there are purposes in which politics play no role)" (2003, p. 107).

Drawing upon her experience with Japanese Buddhism, poet Jane Hirschfield has described "the mind of poetry," and it seems to me that a similar kind of attentive discipline and insight ought to inform and shape place-based education. She claims the core experience is characterized by "the interpenetration of self and Other":

> The nonseparation of Buddhist understanding lies close to the ground of all poetry, Western as well as Eastern. Every metaphor, every description that moves its reader, every hymn-shout of praise, points to the shared existence of beings and things. The mind of poetry makes visible how permeable we are to the winds and moonlight with which we share our house. (1997, pp. 98–99)

As we have seen, Abram has described this sensuous and perceptual reciprocity with the more-than-human world as a "silent conversation between our bodies and things" (1996, p. 49). Utsler, in turn, described being embedded in a tapestry of ecological relationships as "intercorporeality," implying we can never understand the self as inseparable from the more-than-human other (2009). We share our home, within and without.

> To the extent that we are part of the ecology of what-is, our thinking displays the *phusis* of what-is—the fit of response and co-response.
>
> Coming to experience the fit of human thought to the world is a way of finding ourselves at home. (Zwicky, 2003, p. 27).

The Western cultural imperative of corralling meaning into a conduit model of linguistic transaction strictly between humans (and further privileging print-centrism over oral traditions) has severed the identity of thinking from the mind of poetry—severed the understanding of thinking *as* the fit of human thought to the world. Jardine has thus proposed that we *take up* hermeneutics as a kind of ecological imagination in education because: "It wants to listen, to affect and to invite, not merely to inform" (2006, p. 269).

> The task posed to understanding at such a juncture cannot be simply one of corralling that teeming world back into the confines of our constructs.... What addresses us does so from beyond our wanting and doing, beyond our constructs. (p. 271)

One of the critical tasks of ecohermeneutics is recycling what we understand education to be, "what we understand knowledge and tradition and language and conversation and art and play and imagination and words and images and the methods of science to be" (p. 269). An ecohermeneutic education is not "one more damn thing" to throw on the proliferating pile of "sustainable solutions"—it is *not* eco-friendly. There will be sadness and rage, diminishing returns, a sense of loss commensurate with planetary extinction; this is gonna hurt. How we respond is, in a sense, what we understand education to be in an era of ecological emergency. In the end, beyond the verbose theorizing, ecohermeneutics is more like coming to recognize the pedagogic significance of a fistful of red maple leaves, an amanita on the path, a little jar of stones—to hear the questions properly. Not yours, a world's.

অ

> Destiny brought in her collection of stones
> for show & tell.
> *I love them all so much.*
> Teacher did not have to ask many questions
>   every stone, a story.

> Years later, she found the stones in a little jar
> tucked away in that old muted babyblue chest
> with fragments of sea shells & weathered glass.
> Before she tossed them all away, she hesitated
> for a moment
> she held the jar up to her ear &   listened.
>   Nothing. Just dumb rocks.

Chapter Nine

Wittgenstein once claimed: "A poet's words can pierce us." Which, as Zwicky explains, "...what the poet says can point to *this*ness. To the experience of limitless responsibility that is the inner sleeve of love" (2003, p. L58). And, as a reminder, "Good poetry, like all meaningful thought, traces a gesture of address. It enacts ontological attention. Metaphor is one of the means it uses to do this" (2003, p. L58). In this sense, a good education imploys words, metaphors and contemplative practices to co-create and trace the experiences of such gestures, to pierce one with the notion of limitless responsibility to the world via *this* thing-being-event, *here*. Ringing like a little fungi-shaped bell. "*This*ness is the experience of a distinct thing in such a way that the resonant structure of the world sounds through it.... The ontology of *this*ness, of ontological attention and address, has the character of metaphor: its object is, and is not, everything" (2003, p. L55).

> ...the phenomenal experience of *this*ness is not a complex series of relations shading off into the temporally hazy distance. Rather, we are pierced. The *this* strikes into us like a shaft of light. We are focussed by it, and experience it as focussed: what is *this* is unique, it has an utterly distinct—and here notice the sense modality we reach for—flavour or fragrance. (What is important about the metaphor is that it recognizes the object as knowable, but neither visible nor graspable.) (2003, p. L53)

Blenkinsop (2005) offers another means to make sense of the ontology of *this*ness in his examination of Buber. Buber viewed relation as a developmental process, and the pivotal role of the educator was one of "bursting asunder" the culturally contrived and instrumental "I/It relation" to break upon an experience of "I/Thou." An important feature of this bursting asunder, for the ecological educator, is the idea of coming to acknowledge more-than-human alterity as co-teacher (Blenkinsop & Beeman, 2010). Blenkinsop cites several of Buber's early experiences of "deep encounter with the natural world" as having a formative influence on his "relational developmentalism"; in particular, Buber often refers to mystical experience from his book *Daniel*:

> On a gloomy morning I walked upon the highway, saw a piece of mica lying, lifted it up and looked at it for a long time; the day was no longer gloomy, so much light was caught in the stone. And suddenly as I raised my eyes from it, I realized that while I looked I had not been conscious of "object" and "subject"; in my looking the mica and "I" had been one; in looking I had tasted unity.

> I looked at it [the mica] again, the unity did not return. But there it burned in me as though to create. I closed my eyes, I gathered my strength, I bound myself with my object, I raised the mica into the kingdom of the existing. And there,... I first was I. (Buber as cited in Blenkinsop, 2005, p. 288)

Despite the temporality of these mica moments, when Buber looked back upon his life he suggested that such "ecopoetic" (my interpretation, not his) encounters were fundamental in the development of his relational capacity. Which is to say, the *I* becomes more *I* through conscious engagement with the other, not only with human other, but also more-than-human (and according to Buber, "beyond") (Blenkinsop, 2005, p. 288). We become more human through humble consideration and recognition of the shared humus of earthly existence. A moment of *thisness* can be a profound experience in precipitating such an insight; and yet, this ontological dimension rarely features in educational initiatives, ecological or otherwise.

> Buber claimed that, through such things as technology, science and institutionalization, today's world is in a situation of ever increasing "*I/It-ness*," moving farther from relation. Though we live constantly within potential reach of the *Thou* and it is, as Buber said, always 'coming towards us and touching us', yet we "have become inept and uneager for such living intercourse" (Buber, 1970, p. 92). However, there is hope, since "all of these *Thou's* which have been changed into *It's* have it in their nature to change back again into presentness" (Friedman, 1960, p. 63), a change which can be accomplished by learning again to revere the world and its objects. (Blenkinsop, 2005, p. 295)

Although it may seem as though we are left pointing and hoping (Zwicky, 2003) again for spontaneous mica moments to reach out and strike into our educational experiences like shafts of light, at least, with Buber, we have a relational basis that can be consciously developed. For Buber, all humans are born with an ability to relate or what he called an instinct for communion. Abram has similarly claimed, "Humans are tuned for relationship. The eyes, the skin, the tongue, ears, and nostrils—all gates where our body receives the nourishment of otherness" (1996, p. ix). This is promising news for ecologically-minded educators. Although the child is, on the one hand, increasingly inculcated into *I/It-ness* via technology, scientism and institutionalization (read: school); there remains the possibility for education as a free space to revitalize attunement to a caring relation with the natural world informed by experiences of *I/Thou-ness*. Buber saw the teacher in a position not of "making" things happen, but of drawing attention to the world, allowing for the possibility of ecopoetic encounter and, perhaps most importantly, providing support, guidance and understanding when students burst asunder.

> As we have seen, Buber's encounters with the non-human environment were so significant that they shaped him and led him to emphasize similar kinds of encounters for the child in his essay *Education*. However, it was not strictly the encounters that were important, but that the encounters allowed him to see the possibility of relationship and to see the *I* with more clarity. As a result, Buber did not want us to objectify nature, to approach nature in the one-directional monological way of *I/It*, but to understand that any approach to a specific object holds with it the possibility of engaging with the *Eternal Thou*.... This is because the self is discovered and nurtured by means of continually more reflective and conscious relationships, so that the individual becomes a person 'in between' others... (Blenkinsop, 2005, p. 304)

ৡ

"What kind of tree is this?"

The question hangs. Not the mechanical and non-metaphorical aspect of the question—what is the taxonomic category of this organism?—but what does *this* tree with its red lantern-light leaves *mean*?

Begin by inoculating presuppositions with hermeneutic consciousness. Jensen, for example, begins an analysis with a quote from a Canadian lumberman who effectively sums up the worst in the resourcist paradigm: "When I look at trees I see dollar bills" (2002, p. 221). Sit with that for a moment...together. Presuming the relational free space in which to share has already been established, reflect. For me, instant rage, images of the countless clearcuts I have forced myself to traverse, *that* tree, the one I used to sit beside as a child in the park at the end of my street for solace and shade (not it too), collusion, shame, self-loathing. What about you? Where does this come from? What does this mean? Jensen begins to ecocritically deliquesce the resource position by situating it within a cultural-historical context in order to trouble the norm.

> Before we can deforest the planet, we have to change the way we perceive it. Up until five hundred years ago, the people in what we now call North America lived in basic equilibrium with the forests, as part of a complex web of relationships. Then another culture and the beginnings of the industrial system were brought in from the "outside." Before the trees could be cut, they had to be redefined as private or public property. But even before that they had to be redefined as property at all. (p. 221)

As crucially important work as this is, it is nothing new to critically frame perspectives in the context of cultural-historical developments. As Jensen himself has claimed, "I am not the first to remark that our financial riches come at the expense of the planet, those we enslave, our capacity to engage in relationship, and our humanity" (p. 224). So while thoughtful and scholarly ecocritical analysis is key, it must be simultaneously coupled with clearing space to make home for insight.

Now that we are standing out here beneath *this* tree, what kind of practices, resources and disciplines can we draw on to re-think this thing—to consider *this* tree? This is the remedial or ecopoetic capacity of ecohermeneutic work and is, in a sense, much more difficult to facilitate as it cannot be forced and often resists being put into so many words (or remains utterly ineffable). We experience it as something like a shift in the "rhythmic logic" of knowing, something perhaps the body understands in an instant, but it is difficult to translate into categories the mind can deal with or the culture is ready to share.

> The sound of wind in the leaves.
> *My God, I am living in the world!*

Here we are already—precariously so—well beyond prescribed learning outcomes. This will not be on the test, and yet, this is what education is.

ᘔ

In keeping with mycelial mindedness, we might say the deliquescence of calcified epistemic structures enacts a mycoremedial function, reconnecting us to the possibilities of multivocal ways of knowing and revitalizing the grounds for experiences of the living phenomenology of relational eco-constitutionality. This entails the pedagogical development of an ability to see-as, a skill with metaphoric understanding as both a "critical" and "relational" capacity to see what-is over and above our wanting and doing. While it is difficult to trace here in text, the living textures and particularity of *this* tree, perhaps we might further inoculate and respond to a crude instrumental understanding of what a tree means by way of some multivocal poetic and philosophic spawn I gathered.

Begin with a poet, Kahlil Gibran:

> Trees are poems that the earth writes upon the sky. We fell them down and turn them into paper that we may record our emptiness. (2007, p. 178)

Chapter Nine

Sit with this too, and perhaps, record some of your emptiness as an "assignment." Then, weave in some threads from elsewhere, for example, from a beautiful little book entitled *Tree: A Life Story*, by geneticist David Suzuki and science writer Wayne Grady. This story recounts the life of a single five-hundred-year-old Douglas fir and the complex ecological relationships that sustain it. Speaking of trees in the introduction, they have written:

> Rooted securely in the earth, trees reach towards the heavens. All across the planet, trees—in a wonderful profusion of form and function—they literally hold the world together.... Trees are remarkable beings. Yet they stand like extras in life's drama, always there as backdrops to the ever-changing action around them, so familiar and omnipresent that we barely take notice of them. (2007, pp. 1-2)

When do we notice trees? Which trees? Did you ever notice this tree before? Is there a particular tree that stands out in your memory? Why? The concept of foreground and background (recall Plumwood, 1993), particularity, metaphor-rich description—fecund substrates for ecohermeneutic recycling. Then, the conversation takes a turn towards the philosophical with Neil Evernden:

> A tree, we might say, is not so much a thing as a rhythm of exchange, or perhaps a centre of organizational forces. Transpiration induces the upward movement of water and dissolved materials, facilitating an inflow from the soil. If we were aware of this rather than of the appearance of a tree-form, we might regard a tree as a centre of a force-field towards which water is drawn. The object to which we attach significance is the configuration of the forces necessary to being a tree. The visible structure is the indicator that life is happening, just as a dog's bark is an indicator of the existence of that animal. The bark is not the dog any more than the visually delineated object is a tree. We do not mistake the bark for the dog, but we habitually mistake the shape for the tree. Only the visible is regarded as real. It is not necessarily the case that whatever exists must be sharply bounded: in fact, rigid attention to boundaries can obscure the act of being itself. (1993, p. 41)

Being that this is Nuu-chah-nulth territory, we weave in a story by hereditary chief E. Richard Atleo:

> In the Nuu-chah-nulth language, when we speak of the importance of relationships, we also speak of relationships with Wolf, Bear, Deer, and, indeed, with all other life forms for they are all *quu-as*, just like us. Roy Haiyupis, an uncle of mine who served as an elder to the Scientific Panel for Sustainable Forest Practices in Clayoquot Sound, told the story of when, as a boy, his grandfather showed him how to take down a tree. Roy described how his grandfather revered even the bushes and foliage around the tree and treated each with respect. When this paying of respect to the bushes and foliage

was completed, his grandfather lifted up his voice to communicate with the great tree. (2011, pp. 49–50)

Touch the tree, put your hands upon it and listen. David Abram:

> To touch the coarse skin of a tree is thus, at the same time, to experience one's own tactility, to feel oneself touched by the tree...
>
> Walking into a forest, we peer into its green and shadowed depths, listening to the silence of the leaves, tasting the cool and fragrant air. Yet such is the transitivity of perception, the reversibility of the flesh, that we may suddenly feel that the trees are looking at us—we feel ourselves exposed, watched, observed from all sides. If we dwell in this forest for many months, or years, then our experience may shift yet again—we may come to feel that we are a part of this forest, consanguineous with it, and that our experience of the forest is nothing other than the forest experiencing itself. (1996, p. 68)

And finally, we return to Buber and the tree itself, inviting all to consider *this* tree.

> I can look on (a tree) as a picture: stiff column in a shock of light, or splash of green shot with the delicate blue and silver of the background. I can perceive it as movement: flowing veins on clinging, pressing pith, suck of the roots, breathing of the leaves, ceaseless commerce with earth and air—and the obscure growth itself. I can classify it in a species and study it as a type in its structure and mode of life. I can subdue its actual presence and form so sternly that I recognize it only as an expression of law.... I can dissipate it and perpetuate it in number.... In all this the tree remains my object, occupies space and time, and has its nature and constitution. It can, however, also come about, if I have both will and grace, that in considering the tree I become bound up in relation to it. The tree is no longer *It*. I have been seized by the power of exclusiveness. (1970, p. 34)

The shift in "rhythmic logic" from viewing trees as nothing more than dollar bills to Buber's relational attunement will not emerge simply from "getting outside." After all, the Canadian lumberman has surely had ample opportunities—presumably more than most urbanites—to experience the natural world "directly." A relational ontology is a learned and storied discipline, a kind of wisdom requiring not only the ability to see-as, but the will and psychological strength (and, perhaps, something like what Buber would call grace? *Resonance?*) to consider what a tree means "over and above our wanting and doing" (Gadamer, 2004, p. xxvi). This disposition, it seems to me, is best described as an approach to learning that draws upon both the critical and lyrical capacities of poetics to listen to the resonant structures of the world.

Chapter Nine

Listen to this.... The wind whispering between the children's voices rising and falling as the group heads off on a trail to revisit the forest. Left behind, empty, a large box sits quietly in the background on a univocal green sward. The goose, the harbinger of change, sounds above the canopy. The group has returned to witness and experience the seasonal changes of their home. The crispness in the air signifies the need to layer clothing, to fly south, to drop leaves, to hibernate. A few students pause, crouch down...they whisper with their eyes, "look..." (Creeping Snowberry & Blenkinsop, 2010, p. 60)

To repeat: don't think, but look!

references

Abram, D. (1996). *The Spell of the Sensuous: Perception and Language in a More-than-human World.* New York: Vintage Books.

Abram, D. (2010). *Becoming Animal: An Earthly Cosmology.* New York: Pantheon Books.

Alfred, T. (1999). *Peace Power Righteousness: An Indigenous Manifesto.* Don Mills, Ontario: Oxford University Press.

Alfred, T. (2005). *Wasase: Indigenous Pathways of Action and Freedom.* Toronto: University of Toronto Press.

Apple, M. (2009). Controlling the work of teachers. In D. Flinders & S. Thornton (Eds.), *The Curriculum Studies Reader*, 3rd ed. London: Routledge.

Arendt, H. (1969). *Between Past and Future: Eight Exercises in Political Thought.* New York: Penguin Books.

Atleo, E.A. (2001). *Principles of Tsawalk: An Indigenous Approach to Global Crisis.* Vancouver: UBC Press.

Bai, H. (2009). Reanimating the universe: Environmental education and philosophical animism. In M. McKenzie, P. Hart, H. Bai & B. Jickling (Eds.), *Fields of Green: Restorying Culture, Environment and Education.* Cresskill, NJ: Hampton.

Bang, J. & Door, J. (2007). *Language, Ecology, and Society: A Dialectical Approach.* New York: Continuum.

Barfield, R. (2011). *The Ancient Quarrel Between Philosophy and Poetry.* Cambridge: Cambridge University Press.

Bateson, G. (1972). *Steps to an Ecology of Mind.* Chicago: The University of Chicago Press.

Battiste, M. (2013). *Decolonizing Education: Nourishing the Learning Spirit.* Saskatoon: Purich.

BC Ministry of Education. (2007). *Environmental Learning and Experience: An Interdisciplinary Guide for Teachers.* Retrieved April 13, 2011 from http://www.bced.gov.bc.ca/environment-ed/envisust.html

BC Ministry of Education. (2008). *Science Grade 10: An Integrated Resource Package 2008*. Retrieved March 10th, 2012 from http://www.bced.gov.bc.ca/irp/course.php?lang-en&subject-Sciences&course-Science-Grade-10&year-2008

BC Ministry of Education. (2010). *Sustainability Course Content: A Curriculum Framework*. Retrieved March 10th, 2012 from http://www.bced.gov.bc.ca/greenschools/sustcoursecontent.htm

Benjamin, W. (1998). Of language as such and the language of man. In *One-Way Street and Other Writings*. London: Verso.

Bennett, J. (2010). *Vibrant Matter: A Political Ecology of Things*. Durham: Duke University Press.

Bennett, K. (2007). Epistemicide! *The Translator*, 13 (2), 151-169.

Blackner, D. (1993). Education as the normative dimension of philosophical hermeneutics. *Philosophy of Education Yearbook*, 1-9.

Blenkinsop, S. (2005). Martin Buber: Educating for relationship. *Ethics, Place and Environment*. 8 (3), 285-307.

Blenkinsop, S. (2008). Imaginative ecological education: Six necessary components. *Journal for Waldorf/Rudolf Steiner Education*, 10 (2), 16-21.

Blenkinsop, S. (Ed.). (2009). *The Imagination in Education*. Newcastle: Cambridge Scholars.

Blenkinsop, S. (2012). Four slogans for cultural change: An evolving place-based, imaginative, and ecological learning experience. *Journal of Moral Education*, 41 (3), 353-368.

Blenkinsop, S. & Beeman, C. (2008). Dwelling telling: Literalness and ontology. *Paideusis*, 17 (1), 13-24.

Blenkinsop, S. & Beeman, C. (2010). The world as co-teacher: Learning to work with a peerless colleague. *The Trumpeter: Journal of Ecosophy*, 26 (3), 26-39.

Blenkinsop, S. & Fettes, M. (2009). *Aligning Education and Sustainability in Maple Ridge, BC: A Study of Place-Based Ecological Schooling*. Successful SSHRC eCURA Grant Application.

Blenkinsop, S. & Piersol, L. (2013). Listening to the literal: Orientations towards how nature communicates. *Phenomenology & Practice*, 7 (2), 41-60.

Bonnett, M. (2002). Education as a form of the poetic: A Heideggerian approach to learning and the teacher-pupil relationship. In Michael A. Peters (Ed.). *Heidegger, Education, and Modernity*. Lanham, MD: Rowman & Littlefield.

Bonnett, M. (2004). *Retrieving Nature: Education for a Post-humanist Age*. Oxford: Blackwell.

Bowers, C.A. (1993). *Education, Cultural Myths and the Ecological Crisis: Toward Deep Changes*. Albany: SUNY Press.

Bowers, C.A. (1997) *The Culture of Denial: Why the Environmental Movement Needs a Strategy for Reforming Universities and Public Schools*. Albany: State University of New York Press.

Bowers, C.A. (2003). Can critical pedagogy be greened? Retrieved July 24th, 2012 from http://www.cabowers.net/pdf/Can%20CP%20be%20Greened.pdf

Bowers, C.A. (2008a). *Transitions: Educational Reforms That Promote Ecological Intelligence or the Assumptions Underlying Modernity?* University of Oregon Libraries. Retrieved March 10th, 2012 from https://scholarsbank.uoregon.edu/xmlui/handle/1794/3067

Bowers, C.A. (2008b). *Toward a Post-Industrial Consciousness: Understanding the Linguistic Basis of Ecologically Sustainable Educational Reforms*. University of Oregon Libraries. Retrieved March 10th, 2012 from https://scholarsbank.uoregon.edu/xmlui/handle/1794/3067

References

Bowers, C.A. (2009). *Educating for Ecological Intelligence: Practices and Challenges*. University of Oregon Libraries. Retrieved March 10th, 2012 from https://scholarsbank.uoregon.edu/xmlui/handle/1794/3067

Bowers, C.A. & Flinders, D.J. (1990). *Responsive Teaching: An Ecological Approach to Classroom Patterns of Language, Culture and Thought*. New York: Teachers College.

Bowers, C.A. & Martusewicz, R. (2004). The ecojustice dictionary. Retrieved March 10th, 2012 from http://www.ecojusticeeducation.org

Bringhurst, R. (1995). Everywhere being is dancing, knowing is known. In T. Lilburn (Ed.), *Poetry and Knowing*. Kingston, ON: Quarry Press.

Bringhurst, R. (1999). *A Story as Sharp as a Knife: The Classical Haida Mythtellers and Their World*. Lincoln: University of Nebraska Press.

Bringhurst, R. (2002). The philosophy of poetry and the trashing of Doctor Empedokles. In Tim Lilburn (Ed.), *Thinking and Singing: Poetry and the Practice of Philosophy*. Toronto: Cormorant.

Bringhurst, R. (2006). *The Tree of Meaning: Thirteen Talks*. Kentville, NS: Gaspereau.

Bringhurst, R. (2008). *Everywhere Being Is Dancing*. Kentville, NS: Gaspereau.

Buber, M. (1970). *I and Thou*. (W. Kaufmann, Trans.) New York: Charles Scribner's Sons.

Cajete, G. (1994). *Look to the Mountain: An Ecology of Indigenous Education*. Durango, CO: Kivak.

Capra, F. (2002). *The Hidden Connections: Integrating the Biological, Cognitive, and Social Dimensions of Life into a Science of Sustainability*. New York: Doubleday.

Cardinal, H. (1969). *The Unjust Society: The Tragedy of Canada's Indians*. Edmonton: M.G. Hurtig.

Carson, R. (1965). *The Sense of Wonder*. New York: Harper & Row.

Carson, R. (2002). *Silent Spring*. Boston: Houghton Mifflin.

Catton, W.R. (1982). *Overshoot: The Ecological Basis of Revolutionary Change*. Chicago: University of Illinois Press.

Cazeaux, C. (2007). *Metaphor and Continental Philosophy: From Kant to Derrida*. New York: Routledge.

Chamberlin, J.E. (2003). *If This Is Your Land, Where Are Your Stories?: Finding Common Ground*. Toronto: Vintage Canada.

Chambers, C. (1999). A topography for Canadian curriculum theory. *Canadian Journal of Education*, 24 (2), 137-150.

Chambers, C., Hasebe-Ludt, E., Donald, D., Hurren, W., Leggo, C., & Oberg, A. (2008). Métissage. In A. Cole & J. Knowles (Eds.), *Handbook of the Arts in Qualitative Research: Perspectives, Methodologies, Examples and Issues*. Thousand Oaks, CA: Sage.

Chawala, S. (2001). Linguistic and philosophical roots of our environmental crisis. In Alwin Fill & Peter Mühlhäusler (Eds.), *The Ecolinguistics Reader*. New York: Continuum.

Chruikshank, J. (1994). Oral tradition and oral history. Reviewing some issues. *Canadian Historical Review*. LXXV (3), 403-418.

Clouder, C., & Rawson, M. (2003). *Waldorf Education*. Edinburgh: Floris.

Cooper, D. (2005). Heidegger on nature. *Environmental Values*. 14, 339-351.

Creeping Snowberry & Blenkinsop, S. (2010). "Why are those leaves red?": Making sense of the complex symbols: Ecosemiotics in education. *Trumpeter*, 26 (3), 50-60.

Cronon, W. (Ed.). (1995). *Uncommon Ground: Toward Reinventing Nature*. New York: Norton, 1995.

Davis, W. (2009). *Wayfinders: Why Ancient Wisdom Matters in the Modern World*. Toronto: House of Anansi Press.

Debord, G. (1983). *Society of the Spectacle*. London: Rebel Press.

Deluca, K. M. (2005). Thinking with Heidegger: Rethinking environmental theory and practice. *Ethics & the Environment, 10* (1), 67-87.

Denholm, D.S. (2014). *Dead Salmon Dialectics.* Halfmoon Bay, BC: Caitlin.

Denton, D. (1972). *Existential Reflections on Teaching.* North Quincy, MA: Christopher.

Derby, M., Blenkinsop, S., Telford, J., Piersol, L. & Caulkins, M. (2013). Towards resonant, imaginative experiences in ecological and democratic education. *Democracy and Education, 21* (2), 1-5.

Derby, M., Piersol, L., & Blenkinsop, S. (2015). Refusing to settle for pigeons and parks: Urban environmental education in the age of neoliberalism. *Environmental Education Research, 21* (3), 378-389.

Dickinson, M. & Goulet, C. (Eds.). (2010). *Lyric Ecology: An Appreciation of the Works of Jan Zwicky.* Toronto: Cormorant.

Donald, D. (2009). Forts, curriculum, and Indigenous Metissage: Imagining decolonization of Aboriginal-Canadian relations in educational contexts. *First Nations Perspectives, 2* (1), 1-24.

Douglas, G.H. (2007). Heidegger on the education of poets and philosophers. *Educational Theory, 22* (4), 443-459.

Dragland, S. (1995). Introduction: Hunch and hunger. In T. Lilburn (Ed.), *Poetry and Knowing: Speculative Essays and Interviews.* Kingston, Ontario: Quarry, pp. 9-16.

Egan, K. (1987). Literacy and the oral foundations of education. *Harvard Educational Review, 57* (4), 445-472.

Egan, K. (1997). *The Educated Mind: How Cognitive Tools Shape Our Understanding.* Chicago: University of Chicago Press.

Egan, K. (2002). *Getting It Wrong From the Beginning.* New Haven: Yale University Press.

Egan, K. (2005). *An Imaginative Approach to Teaching.* San Francisco: Jossey-Bass.

Egan, K. & Madej, K. (Eds.). (2010). *Engaging Imagination and Developing Creativity in Education.* Newcastle: Cambridge Scholars.

Egan, K. & Nadaner, D. (Eds.). (1988). *Imagination and Education.* New York: Teachers College Press.

Elson, C. (2010). No leading note: A chord for Jan Zwicky. In M. Dickinson & C. Goulet (Eds.), *Lyric Ecology: An Appreciation of the Work of Jan Zwicky.* Toronto: Cormorant.

Emerson, R.W. (1965). *Journals and Miscellaneous Notebooks of Ralph Waldo Emerson, Vol. V: 1835-1838.* London: Oxford University Press.

Emerson, R. W. (1968). *The Complete Works.* Boston: Houghton Mifflin.

Evernden, N. (1993). *The Natural Alien: Humankind and the Environment.* Toronto: University of Toronto Press.

Fawcett, L. (2000). Ethical imagining: Ecofeminist possibilities and environmental learning. *Canadian Journal of Environmental Education, 5,* 134-149.

Fettes, M. (2000). *The Linguistic Ecology of Education.* PhD Dissertation. University of Toronto.

Fettes, M. (2010). The TIEs that bind: How imagination grasps the world. In K. Egan & K. Madej (Eds.), *Engaging Imagination and Developing Creativity in Education.* Newcastle: Cambridge Scholars.

Fettes, M. (2011). Sense and sensibilities: Educating the somatic imagination. *Journal of Curriculum Theorizing, 27* (2), 114-129.

References

Fettes, M. (2013). Imagination and experience: An integrative framework. *Democracy & Education, 21* (1), 1-11.

Fettes, M. & Judson, G. (2011). Imagination and the cognitive tools of place-making. *The Journal of Environmental Education, 42* (2), 123-135.

Fill, A. & Mühlhäusler, P. (Eds.). (2001). *The Ecolinguistics Reader.* New York: Continuum.

Finke, P. (2001). Identity and manifoldness: New perspectives in science, language and politics. In Alwin Fill & Peter Mühlhäusler (Eds.), *The Ecolinguistics Reader.* New York: Continuum.

Fisher-Wirth, A. & Street, L. (Eds.). (2013). *The Ecopoetry Anthology.* San Antonio, Texas: Trinity University Press.

Forbes, J. (2008). *Columbus and Other Cannibals.* New York: Seven Stories.

Foucault, M. (1979). *Discipline and Punish: The Birth of the Prison.* London: Penguin Books.

Foucault, M. (1984). *The Foucault Reader.* New York: Vintage.

Four Arrows. (2013). *Teaching Truly: A Curriculum to Indigenize Mainstream Education.* New York: Peter Lang.

Fox, M. (1983). *Original Blessing.* Santa Fe: Bear and Company.

Friedman, M. (1960). *Martin Buber: The Life of Dialogue.* New York: Harper and Row.

Freire, P. (2006). *Pedagogy of the Oppressed.* New York: Continuum.

Frye, N. (1988). *On Education.* Markham, Ontario: Fitzhenry & Whiteside.

Gadamer, H.G. (1976). *Philosophical Hermeneutics.* D. E. Linge, Trans. Los Angeles: University of California Press.

Gadamer, H.G. (1986). The idea of the university—Yesterday, today, tomorrow. In D. Misgeld & G. Nicholson (Eds. and Trans.), *Hans-Georg Gadamer On Education, Poetry and History: Applied Hermeneutics.* Albany, NY: SUNY Press.

Gadamer, H.G. (1989). *Truth and Method.* J. Weinsheimer, Trans. New York: Continuum Books.

Gadamer, H.G. (1998). *Praise of Theory: Speeches and Essays.* New Haven: Yale University Press.

Gadamer, H.G. (2013). *Truth and Method.* New York: Bloomsbury Academic.

Gajdamaschko, N. (2005). Vygotsky on imagination: Why an understanding of the imagination is an important issue for schoolteachers. *Teaching Education 16* (1), 13-22.

Gallagher, S. (1992). *Hermeneutics and Education.* Albany: State University of New York.

Gatta, J. (2004). *Making Nature Sacred: Literature, Religion, and Environment in America from the Puritans to the Present.* New York: Oxford University Press.

Gibran, K. (2007). *The Collected Works.* New York: Alfred A. Knopf.

Glenn, L. (2010). Resonance, loss. In M. Dickinson & C. Goulet (Eds.), *Lyric Ecology: An Appreciation of the Work of Jan Zwicky.* Toronto: Cormorant.

Gluck, L. (1994). The best American poetry 1993: Introduction. *Proofs & Theories,* New York: Ecco.

Goatly, A. (2000). *Critical Reading and Writing: An Introductory Coursebook.* London: Routledge.

Goddard, H. (1951). *The Meaning of Shakespeare, Vol 1.* Chicago: University of Chicago Press.

Goodbody, A. & Rigby, C.E. (2011). *Ecocritical Theory: New European Approaches.* Charlottesville: University of Virginia Press.

Goodwin, B. (2007). *Nature's Due: Healing Our Fragmented Culture.* Edinburgh: Floris.

Greene, M. (1973). *Teacher as Stranger: Educational Philosophy for the Modern Age.* Belmont, California: Wadsworth Publishing.

Greene, M. (1988). What happened to imagination? In K. Egan & D. Nandner (Eds.), *Imagination and Education.* New York: Teachers College Press.

Greene, M. (1995). *Releasing the Imagination: Essays on Education, the Arts, and Social Change*. San Francisco: Jossey-Bass.

Greenwood, D. (2013). Environment, culture, and education in the anthropocene. In M.P. Mueller, D.J. Tippins, & A.J. Stewart (Eds.), *Assessing Schools for Generation R (Responsibility): A Guide for Legislation and School Policy in Science Education*. New York: Springer.

Gruenewald, D. (2003). The best of both worlds: A critical pedagogy of place. *Educational Researcher. 32* (4), 2-12.

Gruenewald, D. & Manteaw, B.O. (2007). Oil and water still: How No Child Left Behind limits and distorts environmental education in US schools. *Environmental Education Research, 13* (2), 171-188.

Gruenewald, D. & Smith, G.A. (2008). *Place-based Education in the Global Age: Local Diversity*. Mahwah, NJ: Lawrence Erlbaum.

Grun, M. (2005). Gadamer and the otherness of nature: Elements for an environmental education. *Human Studies, 28* (2), 157-171.

Habermas, J. (1990). In D. Rasmussen (Ed.) *Universalism Versus Communitarianism: Contemporary Debates*. Cambridge, MA: MIT Press.

Hampton, E. (1995). Towards a redefinition of Indian education. In M. Battiste & J. Barman (Eds.), *First Nations Education in Canada: The Circle Unfolds*. Vancouver: UBC Press.

Harre, R., Brockmeier, J. & Mühlhäuser, P. (1999). *Greenspeak: A Study of Environmental Discourse*. Thousand Oaks, CA: Sage.

Harris, R. (1981). *The Language Myth*. London: Duckworth

Havelock, E. (1986). *The Muse Learns to Write: Reflections on Orality and Literacy from Antiquity to the Present*. New Haven, CT: Yale University Press.

Heidegger, M. (1962). *Being and Time*. San Francisco: Harper & Row.

Heidegger, M. (1977). The age of the world picture. In *The Question Concerning Technology and Other Essays*. New York: Harper Torchbooks.

Heidegger, M. (1993). The question concerning technology. In D. F. Krell (Ed.), *Martin Heidegger: Basic Writings*. San Francisco: Harper Collins, pp. 311-42.

Heidegger, M. (1999). *Contributions to Philosophy: Of the Event*. Bloomington: Indiana University Press.

Heidegger, M. (2001). *Poetry, Language, Thought*. New York: Harper & Row.

Hirschfield, J. (1997). *Nine Gates: Entering the Mind of Poetry*. New York: Harper Collins.

Huckle, J. & Wals, A.E.J. (2015). The UN Decade of Education for Sustainable Development: Business as usual in the end. *Environmental Education Research, 21* (3), 491-505.

Hughes, T. (1988). Myth and education. In Kieran Egan & Dan Nadaner (Eds.), *Imagination and Education*. New York: Teachers College.

Hursh, D. & Henderson, J. (2011). Contesting global neoliberalism and creating alternative futures. *Discourse: Studies in the Cultural Politics of Education, 32* (2), 171-185.

Hursh, D., Henderson, J. & Greenwood, D. (2015). Environmental education in a neoliberal climate. *Environmental Education Research, 21* (3), 299-318.

Illich, I. (1971). *Deschooling Society*. New York: Harper & Row.

Illich, I. (1980). Vernacular values. *Philosophica, 26*, 47-102.

Jardine, D. (1998). *To Dwell with a Boundless Heart: Essays in Curriculum Theory, Hermeneutics, and the Ecological Imagination*. New York: Peter Lang.

References

Jardine, D. (2006). On hermeneutics: "Over and above our wanting and doing." In K. Tobin & J. Kincheloe (Eds.), *Doing Educational Research: A Handbook*. Rotterdam: Sense, pp. 269-288.

Jardine, D. (2012). *Pedagogy Left in Peace*. New York: Continuum.

Jensen, D. (2002). *The Culture of Make Believe*. New York: Context.

Jensen, D. (2004). *A Language Older Than Words*. White River Junction, VT: Chelsea Green.

Jensen, D. (2006). *Endgame, Vol 1: The Problem of Civilization*. New York: Seven Stories Press.

Jensen, D. & McBay, E. (2009). *What We Leave Behind*. New York: Seven Stories.

Joldersma, C. (2009). How can science help us care for nature? Hermeneutics, fragility, and responsibility for the Earth. *Educational Theory, 59* (4), 465-483.

Judson, G. (2010). *A New Approach to Ecological Education*. New York: Peter Lang.

Judson, G. (2015). *Engaging Imagination in Ecological Education: Practical Strategies for Teaching*. Vancouver: Pacific Educational.

Kahn, R. (2010). *Critical pedagogy, ecoliteracy and planetary crisis*. New York: Peter Lang.

Kelly, V. (2012). A Métis manifesto. In C. Chambers, E. Hasebe-Ludt, C. Leggo, & A. Sinner, (Eds.), *A Heart of Wisdom: Life Writing as Empathetic Inquiry*. New York: Peter Lang.

Kheel, M. (2008). *Nature Ethics: An Ecofeminist Perspective*. Lanham, MD: Rowman & Littlefield.

Kincheloe, J. (2010). *Knowledge and Critical Pedagogy: An Introduction*. New York: Springer.

Kingsnorth, P. (2013) Dark ecology: Searching for truth in a post-green world. *Orion*, January/February, 18-29.

Koch, T. (1995). Interpretive approaches in nursing research: The influence of Husserl and Heidegger. *Journal of Advanced Nursing. 21*, 827-836.

Koepnick, L. (1999). *Walter Benjamin and the Aesthetics of Power*. Lincoln, NE: University of Nebraska.

Kolbert, E. (2014). *The Sixth Extinction: An Unnatural History*. New York: Henry Holt.

Kulnieks, A. (2008). *Ecopoetics and the Epistemology of Landscape: Interpreting Indigenous and Latvian Ancestral Ontologies*. Unpublished doctoral thesis, York University, Toronto, ON.

Kulnieks, A., Longboat, D.R., & Young, K. (2010). Re-indigenizing curriculum: An eco-hermeneutic approach to learning. *AlterNative: An International Journal of Indigenous Peoples*. 6 (1), 15-24.

Latour, B. (1993). *We Have Never Been Modern*. Cambridge, MA: Harvard University Press.

Latour, B. (2009). Will non-humans be saved? An argument in ecotheology. *Journal of the Royal Anthropological Institute. 15* (3), 459-475.

Lear, L. (1997). *Rachel Carson: Witness for Nature*. New York: Henry Holt.

Lechevrel, N. (2009, June). The intertwined histories of ecolinguistics and ecological approaches of language(s). Symposium on Ecolinguistics-Ecology of Science, University of Southern Denmark, Odense Institute of Language and Communication.

Lee, D. (2002). Body music: Notes on rhythm in poetry. In Tim Lilburn (Ed.), *Thinking and Singing: Poetry and the Practice of Philosophy*. Toronto: Cormorant.

Lee, D. (2010). The music of thinking. In M. Dickinson & C. Goulet (Eds.), *Lyric Ecology: An Appreciation of the Work of Jan Zwicky*. Toronto: Cormorant.

Lewis, T. & Kahn, R. (2010). *Education out of Bounds: Reimagining Cultural Studies for a Posthuman Age*. New York: Palgrave Macmillan.

Lilburn, T. (Ed.). (1995). *Poetry and Knowing: Speculative Essays and Interviews*. Kingston, Ontario: Quarry.

Lilburn, T. (Ed.). (2002). *Thinking and Singing: Poetry and the Practice of Philosophy*. Toronto: Cormorant.

Lilburn, T. (2008a). *Going Home*. Toronto: House of Anansi.

Lilburn, T. (2008b). The horse hitting its stride: An interview with Tim Lilburn. *The Malahat Review*, Winter 165, 18-30.

Longboat, D.R. (1999). The tree. In The Haudenosaunee Environmental Task Force (Eds.), *The Words Which Come Before All Else*. Cornwall Island, Akwesasne: Native North American Travelling College Press.

Louv, R. (2008). *Last Child in the Woods: Saving Our Children from Nature-Deficit Disorder*. Chapel Hill, NC: Algonquin Books of Chapel Hill.

Macy, J. & Brown, M.Y. (1998). *Coming Back to Life: Practices to Reconnect Our Lives, Our World*. Gabriola Island, BC: New Society.

Maracle, L. (1996). *I Am Woman: A Native Perspective on Sociology and Feminism*. Vancouver: Press Gang.

Martusewicz, R. (2014). Letting our hearts break: On facing the "hidden wound" of human supremacy. *Canadian Journal of Environmental Education*, 19, 31-46.

Martusewicz, R. & Edmundson, J. (2004). Social foundations as pedagogies of responsibility and eco-ethical commitment. In D. Butin (Ed.), *Teaching Context: A Primer for the Social Foundations of Education*. Mahwah, NJ: Lawrence Erlbaum.

Martusewicz, R., Edmundson, J. & Lupinacci, J. (2011). *Ecojustice Education*. New York: Routledge.

McKay, D. (2002). The bushtits' nest. In Tim Lilburn (Ed.), *Thinking and Singing: Poetry and the Practice of Philosophy*. Toronto: Cormorant.

McKenzie, M. (2005). The 'post-post period' and environmental education research. *Environmental Education Research*, 11 (4), 401-412.

McKenzie, M. (2012). Education for y'all: Global neoliberalism and the case for a politics of scale in sustainability education policy. *Policy Futures in Education*, 10 (2), 165-177.

McKenzie, M., Bieler, A., & McNeil, R. (2015). Education policy mobility. Reimagining sustainability in neoliberal times. *Environmental Education Research*, 21 (3), 319-337.

McKenzie, M., Hart, P., Bai, H., & Jickling, B. (Eds.). (2009). *Fields of Green: Restorying Culture, Environment, and Education*. Cresskill, NJ: Hampton.

McKibben, B. (1999). *The End of Nature*. New York: Anchor.

Merchant, C. (1980). *The Death of Nature: Women, Ecology, and the Scientific Revolution*. San Francisco: Harper & Row.

Merleau-Ponty, M. (1969). *The Visible and the Invisible*. Evanston, IL: Northwestern University Press.

Merleau-Ponty, M. (2008). *Phenomenology of Perception*. London: Routledge.

Michelfelder, D. & Palmer, R. (Eds.). (1989). *Dialogue and Deconstruction: The Gadamer-Derrida Encounter*. Albany: State University of New York.

Moldenhauer, J. (1990). "Walden" and Wordsworth's Guide to the English Lake District. *Studies in the American Renaissance*. 261-292.

Moore, P. (2014). *Confessions of a Greenpeace Dropout: The Making of a Sensible Environmentalist*. Vancouver: Beatty Street.

Morgan, A. (1995). *Toads and Toadstools: The Natural History, Folklore and Cultural Oddities of a Strange Association*. Berkeley, CA: Celestial Arts.

References

Morton, T. (2010) *The Ecological Thought*. Cambridge, MA: Harvard University Press.

Mueller-Vollmer, K. (1994). *The Hermeneutics Reader: Texts of the German Tradition from the Enlightenment to the Present*. New York: Continuum.

Nielsen, T., Fitzgerald, R. & Fettes, M. (2010). (Eds.). *Imagination in Educational Theory and Practice: A Many-sided Vision*. Newcastle: Cambridge Scholars.

Orr, D. (1991). What is education for? *The Learning Revolution*, Winter, 52–58.

Orr, D. (2005). Recollection. In M.K. Stone & Z. Barlow (Eds.), *Ecological Literacy: Educating Our Children for a Sustainable World*. San Francisco: Sierra Club.

Paraskeva, J.M. (2011). *Conflicts in Curriculum Theory: Challenging Hegemonic Epistemologies*. New York: Palgrave Macmillan.

Pierce, C. (2013). *Education in the Age of Biocapitalism: Optimizing Educational Life for a Flat World*. New York: Palgrave Macmillan.

Piercey, R. (2004). Ricoeur's account of tradition and the Gadamer-Habermas debate. *Human Studies, 27* (3), 259–280.

Plumwood, V. (1993). *Feminism and the Mastery of Nature*. London: Routledge.

Plumwood, V. (2002). *Environmental Culture: The Ecological Crisis of Reason*. New York: Routledge.

Prakash, M.S. (2009). Soil, seeds, salt: Education brought down to Earth. *Yes! Magazine*. Retrieved from http://www.yesmagazine.org/issues/learn-as-you-go/soil-seeds-salt-education-brought-down-to-earth

Prakash, M.S. & Esteva, G. (1998). *Grassroots Postmodernism: Remaking the Soils of Culture*. New York: Zed.

Prakash, M.S. & Esteva, G. (2008). *Escaping Education: Living as Learning within Grassroots Cultures*. New York: Peter Lang.

Rasmussen, D. (2011). Some honest talk about Non-Indigenous education. *Our Schools, Our Selves, 20* (2), 19–33.

Rautio, P. (2013). Being nature: Interspecies articulation as a species- specific practice of relating to environment. *Environmental Education Research, 19* (4), 445–457.

Ricoeur, P. (1991). *From Text to Action: Essays in Hermeneutics II*. Trans. by Kathleen Blamey and John B. Thompson. Evanston: Northwestern University Press.

Ricoeur, P. (1992). *Oneself as Another*. Trans. By Kathleen Blamey, Chicago: University of Chicago Press.

Rose, E. (2013). *On Reflection: An Essay on Technology, Education and the Status of Thought in the Twenty-First Century*. Toronto: Canadian Scholars'.

Russell, C.L. (2005). 'Whoever does not write is written': The role of 'nature' in post-post approaches to environmental education research. *Environmental Education Research*, 11 (4), 433–443.

Russell, C.L. & Bell, A.C. (1996). A politicized ethic of care: Environmental education from an ecofeminist perspective. In K. Warren (Ed.), *Women's Voices in Experiential Education*. Dubuque, IA: Kendall Hunt, pp. 172–181.

Sacks, S. (Ed.) (1978). *On Metaphor*. Chicago: The University of Chicago Press.

Sakolsky, R. & Koehnline, J. (Eds.). (1993). *Gone to Croatan: Origins of North American Drop-Out Culture*. New York: Autonomedia.

Sammel, A. (2003). An invitation to dialogue: Gadamer, hermeneutic phenomenology, and critical environmental education. *Canadian Journal of Environmental Education*. 8, Spring, 155–168.

Sanger, P. (2010). Almost blind with light. In M. Dickinson & C. Goulet (Eds.), *Lyric Ecology: An Appreciation of the Work of Jan Zwicky*. Toronto: Cormorant.

Schultes, R.E., & Hofmann, A. (1987). *Plants of the Gods: Origins of Hallucinogenic Use*. New York: A. van der Marck.

Seidel, J. (2014). Reading the stones. In J. Seidel & D.W. Jardine (Eds.), *Ecological Pedagogy, Buddhist Pedagogy, Hermeneutic Pedagogy*. New York: Peter Lang.

Seidel, J. & Jardine, D. (2014). *Ecological Pedagogy, Buddhist Pedagogy, Hermeneutic Pedagogy*. New York: Peter Lang.

Serres, M. (2010). *Malfeasance: Appropriation Through Pollution?* Redwood City, CA: Stanford University Press.

Shepard, P. (1982). *Nature and Madness*. Athens, GA: University of Georgia Press.

Sheridan, J. & Longboat, D. (2006). The Haudenosaunee imagination and the ecology of the sacred. *Space and Culture*, 9 (4), 365-381.

Shiva, V. (2005). *Earth Democracy: Justice, Sustainability and Peace*. Cambridge, MA: South End.

Simic, C. (1990). *Wonderful Words, Silent Truth: Essays on Poetry and a Memoir*. Ann Arbor: The University of Michigan Press.

Sinclair, S. (2010). Wisdom. In M. Dickinson & C. Goulet (Eds.), *Lyric Ecology: An Appreciation of the Work of Jan Zwicky*. Toronto: Cormorant.

Skinner, J. (2001). *ecopoetics*, no.1. Buffalo, NY: Periplum.

Smith, D.G. (1988). From logocentrism to rhysomatics: Working through the boundary police to a new love. Paper presented at the Bergamo Conference on Curriculum Theory and Classroom Practice, Dayton, Ohio.

Smith, D.G. (1991). Hermeneutic inquiry: The hermeneutic imagination and the pedagogic text. In E. Short (Ed.), *Forms of Curriculum Inquiry*. Albany, NY: State University of New York Press.

Smith, D.G. (1999). *Pedagon: Interdisciplinary Essays in the Human Sciences, Pedagogy, and Culture*. New York: Peter Lang.

Smith, D.G. (2003). *The Mission of the Hermeneutic Scholar: Essays in Honour of Nelson Haggerson*. New York: Peter Lang.

Smith, M. (2001a). *An Ethics of Place: Radical Ecology, Postmodernity, and Social Theory*. Albany: State University of New York Press.

Smith, M. (2001b). Lost for words? Gadamer and Benjamin on the nature of language and the 'language' of nature. *Environmental Values*. 10, 59-75.

Smith, M. (2007). Wild-life: Anarchy, ecology, and ethics. *Environmental Politics*. 16 (3), 470-487.

Snyder, G. (1980). *The Real Work*. New York: New Directions.

Stamets, P. (2005). *Mycelium Running: How Mushrooms Can Help Save the World*. Berkeley, CA: Ten Speed.

Steffensen, S.V. (Ed.). (2007). *Language, Ecology and Society*. New York: Continuum.

Steffensen, S.V. & Fill, A. (2014). Ecolinguistics: The state of the art and future horizons. *Language Sciences*, 41, 6-25.

Stibbe, A. (2012). *Animals Erased: Discourse, Ecology and Reconnection with the Natural World*. Middletown, CT: Wesleyan University Press.

Stibbe, A. (n.d.). The Language and Ecology Research Forum. Retrieved October 17, 2014 from http://www.ecoling.net

References

Sustainability and Education Policy Network. (2014). Retrieved from http://sepn.ca. Saskatoon: University of Saskatchewan.
Suzuki, D.T & Grady, W. (2007). *Tree: A Life Story.* Vancouver: Greystone Books.
Taylor, T. & Davis, H. (Eds.). (1990). *Redefining Linguistics.* New York: Routledge.
Tuck, E. & McKenzie, M. (2015). *Place in Research: Theory, Methodology and Methods.* New York: Routledge.
Tuck, E. & Yang, K.W. (2012). Decolonization is not a metaphor. *Decolonization: Indigeneity, Education and Society, 1* (1), 1-40.
Tupper, K. (2002). Entheogens and existential intelligence: The use of plant teachers as cognitive tools. *Canadian Journal of Education, 27* (4), 499-516.
Usher, R. & Edwards, R. (1994). *Postmodernism and Education: Different Voices, Different Worlds.* New York: Routledge.
Utsler, D. (2009). Paul Ricoeur's hermeneutics as a model for environmental philosophy. *Philosophy Today.* Summer, 173-178.
van Buren, J. (1995). Critical environmental hermeneutics. *Environmental Ethics. 17* (3), 259-275.
Vizenor, G. (1970). *Anishnabe Adisokan: Tales of the People.* Minneapolis: Nodin.
Vygotsky, L. (1978). *Mind in Society: The Development of Higher Psychological Processes.* Cambridge, MA: Harvard University Press.
Vygotsky, L. (1986). *Thought and Language.* (Alex Kozulin, Trans.). Cambridge, MA: MIT Press.
Vygotsky, L. (2004). Imagination and creativity in childhood. *Journal of Russian and East European Psychology. 42* (1), 7-97.
Waddington, T. & Johnson, J. (2010). Imaginative education and the national framework for values education in Australian schools: Practical implementations for promoting ethical understanding. *International Research Handbook on Values Education and Student Wellbeing, Part 2,* 559-577.
Weil, S. (1952). *Gravity and Grace.* New York: Putnam.
Weil, S. (1970). *First and Last Notebooks.* (Richard Rees, Trans.). London: Oxford University Press.
Weil, S. (1974). *Cahiers,* Vol. 3. Paris: Plon.
White, L. (1967). The historical roots or our ecological crisis. *Science, 155,* 1203-1207.
Wittgenstein, L. (1980). *Remarks on the Philosophy of Psychology, Vol 1.* (C.G. Luckhardt & M.A.E. Aue, Trans.). Oxford: Basil Blackwell.
Wittgenstein, L. (1982). *Last Writings on the Philosophy of Psychology,* Vol. 1. (C.G. Luckhardt & M.A.E. Aue, Trans.). Chicago: University of Chicago Press.
Wittgenstein, L. (1984). *Culture and Value.* (Peter Winch, Trans.). Chicago: University of Chicago Press.
Wittgenstein, L. (1993). Philosophy. (C.G. Luckhardt & M.A.E. Aue, Trans.). *Philosophical Occasions 1912-1951.* James Klagge & Alfred Nordmann (Eds.). Cambridge: Hackett.
Wittgenstein, L. (2007). *Zettel.* G.E.M. Anscombe & G. H. von Wright (Eds.). Los Angeles: Basil Blackwell.
Wittgenstein, L. (2009). *Philosophical Investigations.* Rev 4th ed. by P.M.S. Hacker and Joachim Schulte. (G.E.M. Anscombe, P.M.S. Hacker and Joachim Schulte, Trans.). Chichester, West Sussex: Wiley-Blackwell.
Wright, R. (2004). *A Short History of Progress.* Toronto: House of Anansi.

Young, K. (2007). Environmental education leadership and its origins. In W. Smale & K. Young (Eds.), *Approaches to Educational Leadership*. Calgary, AB: Detselig.

Zimmerman, M. (1983). Toward a Heideggerian ethos for radical environmentalism, *Environmental Ethics* 5 (2): 99-132.

Zinn, H. (1999). *A People's History of the United States*. New York: Harper Collins.

Zwicky, J. (1986). *Wittgenstein Elegies*. Ilderton, Ontario: Brick.

Zwicky, J. (1992). *Lyric Philosophy*. Toronto: University of Toronto Press.

Zwicky, J. (1995). Bringhurst's Presocratics: Lyric and ecology. In T. Lilburn (Ed.), *Poetry and Knowing: Speculative Essays and Interviews*. Kingston, Ontario: Quarry Press.

Zwicky, J. (1998). *Songs for Relinquishing the Earth*. London, Ont.: Brick.

Zwicky, J. (2002a). Once upon a time in the west: Heidegger and the poets. In Tim Lilburn (Ed.), *Thinking and Singing: Poetry and the Practice of Philosophy*. Toronto: Cormorant.

Zwicky, J. (2002b). Dream logic and the politics of interpretation. In Tim Lilburn (Ed.), *Thinking and Singing: Poetry and the Practice of Philosophy*. Toronto: Cormorant.

Zwicky, J. (2003). *Wisdom & Metaphor*. Kentville, N.S.: Gaspereau.

Zwicky, J. (2008). Lyric realism: Nature poetry, silence and ontology. *The Malahat Review, 165* (Winter), 85-91.

Zwicky, J. (2012). What is ineffable? *International Studies in the Philosophy of Science, 26* (2), 197-217.

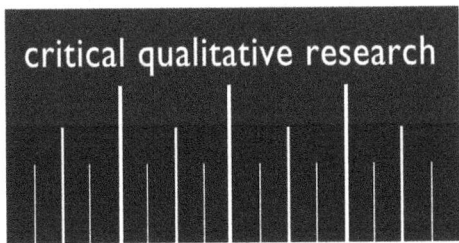

critical qualitative research

Shirley R. Steinberg and Gaile S. Cannella, *General Editors*

The Critical Qualitative Research series examines societal structures that oppress and exclude so that transformative actions can be generated. This transformed research is activist in orientation. Because the perspective accepts the notion that nothing is apolitical, research projects themselves are critically examined for power orientations, even as they are used to address curricular, educational, or societal issues.

This methodological work challenges modernist orientations and universalist impositions, asking critical questions like: Who/what is heard? Who/what is silenced? Who is privileged? Who is disqualified? How are forms of inclusion and exclusion being created? How are power relations constructed and managed? How do different forms of privilege and oppression intersect to affect educational, societal, and life possibilities for various individuals and groups?

We are particularly interested in manuscripts that offer critical examinations of curriculum, policy, public communities, and the ways in which language, discourse practices, and power relations prevent more just transformations.

For additional information about this series or for the submission of manuscripts, please contact:
  Shirley R. Steinberg and Gaile S. Cannella
  msgramsci@gmail.com | gaile.cannella@gmail.com

To order other books in this series, please contact our Customer Service Department:
  (800) 770-LANG (within the U.S.)
  (212) 647-7706 (outside the U.S.)
  (212) 647-7707 FAX

Or browse online by series:
  www.peterlang.com

www.ingramcontent.com/pod-product-compliance
Ingram Content Group UK Ltd.
Pitfield, Milton Keynes, MK11 3LW, UK
UKHW022239230426